Lawmen
of the
Old West

By Dwayne Epstein

LUCENT BOOKS

An imprint of Thomson Gale, a part of The Thomson Corporation

THOMSON

™

GALE

Detroit • New York • San Francisco • San Diego • New Haven, Conn.
Waterville, Maine • London • Munich

© 2005 Thomson Gale, a part of The Thomson Corporation.

Thomson and Star Logo are trademarks and Gale and Lucent Books are registered trademarks used herein under license.

For more information, contact
Lucent Books
27500 Drake Rd.
Farmington Hills, MI 48331-3535
Or you can visit our Internet site at http://www.gale.com

LIBRARY OF CONGRESS CATALOGING-IN-PUBLICATION DATA

Epstein, Dwayne.
    Lawmen of the Old West / by Dwayne Epstein.
        p. cm. — (History makers)
    Includes bibliographical references and index.
    ISBN 1-59018-560-9 (alk. paper)
    1. Peace officers—West (U.S.)—Biography—Juvenile literature. 2. Frontier and pioneer life—West (U.S.)—Juvenile literature. 3. West (U.S.)—History—1860–1890—Juvenile literature. I. Title. II. Series.
    F594.E67 2004
    978'.02'0922—dc22
                                                                              2004010690

Printed in the United States of America

CONTENTS

FOREWORD

The literary form most often referred to as "multiple biography" was perfected in the first century A.D. by Plutarch, a perceptive and talented moralist and historian who hailed from the small town of Chaeronea in central Greece. His most famous work, *Parallel Lives*, consists of a long series of biographies of noteworthy ancient Greek and Roman statesmen and military leaders. Frequently, Plutarch compares a famous Greek to a famous Roman, pointing out similarities in personality and achievements. These expertly constructed and very readable tracts provided later historians and others, including playwrights like Shakespeare, with priceless information about prominent ancient personages and also inspired new generations of writers to tackle the multiple biography genre.

The Lucent History Makers series proudly carries on the venerable tradition handed down from Plutarch. Each volume in the series consists of a set of five to eight biographies of important and influential historical figures who were linked together by a common factor. In *Rulers of Ancient Rome*, for example, all the figures were generals, consuls, or emperors of either the Roman Republic or Empire; while the subjects of *Fighters Against American Slavery*, though they lived in different places and times, all shared the same goal, namely, the eradication of human servitude. Mindful that politicians and military leaders are not (and never have been) the only people who shape the course of history, the editors of the series have also included representatives from a wide range of endeavors, including scientists, artists, writers, philosophers, religious leaders, and sports figures.

Each book is intended to give a range of figures—some well known, others less known; some who made a great impact on history, others who made only a small impact. For instance, by making Columbus's initial voyage possible, Spain's Queen Isabella I, featured in *Women Leaders of Nations*, helped to open up the New World to exploration and exploitation by the European powers. Inarguably, therefore, she made a major contribution to a series of events that had momentous consequences for the entire world. By contrast, Catherine II, the eighteenth-century Russian queen, and Golda Meir, the modern Israeli prime minister, did not play roles of global impact; however, their policies and actions significantly influenced the historical development of both their own

4

countries and their regional neighbors. Regardless of their relative importance in the greater historical scheme, all of the figures chronicled in the History Makers series made contributions to posterity; and their public achievements, as well as what is known about their private lives, are presented and evaluated in light of the most recent scholarship.

In addition, each volume in the series is documented and substantiated by a wide array of primary and secondary source quotations. The primary source quotes enliven the text by presenting eyewitness views of the times and culture in which each history maker lived, while the secondary source quotes, taken from the works of respected modern scholars, offer expert elaboration and/or critical commentary. Each quote is footnoted, demonstrating to the reader exactly where biographers find their information. The footnotes also provide the reader with the means of conducting additional research. Finally, to further guide and illuminate readers, each volume in the series features photographs, two bibliographies, and a comprehensive index.

The History Makers series provides both students engaged in research and more casual readers with informative, enlightening, and entertaining overviews of individuals from a variety of circumstances, professions, and backgrounds. No doubt all of them, whether loved or hated, benevolent or cruel, constructive or destructive, will remain endlessly fascinating to each new generation seeking to identify the forces that shaped their world.

Neither Saints nor Sinners

The American West of the nineteenth century has been the foundation for countless tales, both factual and fictionalized, that have been central in forming the image of the lawman of this romanticized period. Writers of cheap novels of the time created the image of the courageous and virtuous lawman pitted virtually alone against an onslaught of immoral criminals. In the twentieth century, historians have sought to revise that image with tales of these same lawmen indulging in self-serving immorality. The truth is that more often than not these individuals were neither saints nor sinners, but men from all walks of life who tried as best they could to uphold the laws of their communities. If there is a common thread among these individuals, it is that they were neither the icons of virtue that legend has painted them nor the extreme opposite, as often portrayed by revisionists.

Some Legendary Lawmen

Known as the "Hanging Judge," Isaac C. Parker's tough stance on crime was accomplished not with firearms, but by bringing justice to a lawless area known as "Robber's Roost." Before his arrival as the first federal judge in the area that is now mostly Oklahoma, Parker's jurisdiction was rife with criminal activity. The court was located in Fort Smith, Arkansas, but before Parker's arrival, a popular slogan warned, "There is no law west of St. Louis and no god west of Fort Smith."[1] Parker's twenty-year tenure presiding over Fort Smith permanently altered that viewpoint and made eventual statehood for Oklahoma possible.

Many lawmen simply drifted into the profession and made a name for themselves whether they liked it or not. Wyatt Earp never intended to be a lawman, especially one of the most controversial lawmen of all time. As a lawman in both Kansas and Arizona, he exhibited coolness under pressure in handling the cowboys who rode roughshod into town at the end of the trail. However, the event he is most remembered for, the legendary gunfight at the O.K. Corral, and its aftermath, left him a fugitive from justice and an American legend.

Though a surprising number of lawmen had been on the opposite side of the law in their early years, few went to such extremes as both criminal and lawman as Frank Canton did. Born Joe Horner, he committed robbery and even murder before he was finally captured. He escaped from jail and later reemerged as Frank Canton, a lawman almost unparalleled in his pursuit of outlaws of the day. His knowledge of the way frontier criminals operated astounded his superiors. Central to the infamous Johnson County War between ranchers and settlers in Wyoming, Canton also successfully pursued criminals in Oklahoma and Alaska. He became Oklahoma's first adjutant general, organizing the state's National Guard. When he died, few of the dignitaries present at his funeral were aware of the deceased's real name, let alone his shady deeds.

The Value of Reputation

Bringing an end to the career of a legendary outlaw was also an important contribution to taming the frontier. The life and bloody career of the most infamous outlaw of the Old West, Billy the Kid, were ended by New Mexico sheriff Pat Garrett. Garrett's life was forever altered by this one momentous event, as the specter of Billy the Kid's death seemed to taint all his future endeavors. His attempts to remain a lawman and then to become a rancher proved unsuccessful. His life ended in an act of murder for which the alleged killer was cleared of all charges. In spite of his attempts to move on with his life, being "the man who killed Billy the Kid" remained Pat Garrett's legacy.

Oftentimes it is not the reality of a situation that gains a lawman his reputation, but the way in which it is perceived. The high points of Bat Masterson's awe-inspiring reputation as a buffalo hunter, army scout, lawman, gunfighter, gambler, and sportsman were largely his own creation. Touted as having killed more than two dozen men, Masterson could enter any public place and command unwavering respect. He utilized this respect to maintain the peace, but in truth, much of what was said about him in his own time was an exaggeration of the facts. It is questionable whether Masterson ever killed anyone. He did, however, prove that a lawman's reputation was of the utmost importance in maintaining law and order.

The Man Behind the Badge

Bill Tilghman is not as well known as Wyatt Earp or Bat Masterson, but in his five-decade career as a lawman, his deeds surpassed those of his more famous counterparts. He cleaned up the remnants of crime in Dodge City; captured Bill Doolin, the last great outlaw of the West; and even directed a silent film to honestly portray the sheriff of the West. At the age of seventy, Tilghman came out of retirement to tackle the lawlessness of Prohibition that swept through an Oklahoma boomtown. In his lifetime, the West changed from wild frontier to modern mecca, but there was always the threat of criminal behavior. Tilghman continued his battle against this behavior until his death at the hands of a corrupt federal officer.

All these men, while fallible, had the qualities required of legendary lawmen. They had the courage to control mobs of drunken and dangerous cowhands, the determination to trail a killer or an outlaw band for weeks in order to bring them to justice, and the integrity to ignore bribes and resist the pressure of local politicians and fickle community leaders. Regardless of their faults, these lawmen exhibited remarkable courage, determination, and integrity in the execution of their duties.

CHAPTER 1

Why the West Was Wild

The period from the end of the Civil War to the early 1900s was a time of immense change in the American West. Several cultural and technological developments, such as the creation of more convenient and deadly firearms and the mass consumption of alcohol, greatly influenced the often extreme behavior of settlers in the West. The result was often tragic when people with wildly divergent histories came into direct conflict with each other amid the wagon trains, railroads, and cattle drives that crisscrossed the West.

A western lawman had to contend with a wide variety of conflicts among frontier factions. Cattlemen and sheepmen vied for land rights. Landowners and settlers competed for control of precious frontier real estate. A handful of notorious outlaws terrorized the

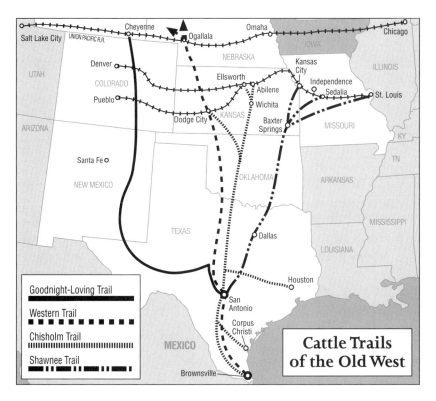

Goodnight-Loving Trail

Western Trail

Chisholm Trail

Shawnee Trail

Cattle Trails of the Old West

frontier in their attempt to find easy riches. Racial tensions between whites, Native Americans, Mexicans, and other races frequently exploded into vigilantism and violence. Southerners and Northerners still holding a grudge after the Civil War were known to lash out at each other when provoked. A lawman had to be tough enough, and resourceful enough, to deal with such volatile situations.

Different Places, Different Problems

Different geographic regions also meant different challenges for lawmen, based on the given territory of the western frontier. Many of the legendary lawmen of the West gained their status dealing with the troubles that arose in the cow towns of Kansas. From 1867 until 1888, Texas cowboys drove their cattle north along the trail into the freight yards awaiting their cargo in Abilene, Ellsworth, Wichita, and, the most famous of them all, Dodge City. With so much livestock present, horse thievery and cattle rustling became common criminal activities.

The western cowboy was a unique breed from which evolved one of the icons of the frontier, the gunslinger. Known in their day as shootists, mankillers, or sometimes just bad men (the terms "gunslinger" or "gunfighter" are strictly twentieth-century terms), these men achieved notoriety and celebrity by killing without getting killed. The saloons, brothels, and dance halls of Dodge City became the most popular proving grounds of the West. A popular anecdote at the time illustrates Dodge City's reputation:

> A drunken cowboy got aboard a Santa Fe train at Newton [Kansas]. When the conductor asked him for the fare, the cowpuncher handed him a handful of money. "Where do you want to go?" asked the conductor.
>
> "To Hell," replied the cowboy.
>
> "Well, give me $2.50 and get off at Dodge."[2]

Keeping the peace in a western cow town was a complex task. If cowboys became too rowdy in their celebrations, lawmen were not always able to restore order. But cowboys were an important part of a town's economic well-being. When they came to town with money to spend—usually a lump sum that they were paid at the end of a seasonal cattle drive—they added considerably to a town's coffers. To remove the cowboy presence from a town would also mean losing the business of large cattle companies. Western historian Robert R. Dykstra aptly summed up this conflict: "The problem for the cattle town people was not to rid themselves of visitors prone to violence but to suppress the violence while retaining the visitors."[3]

Another region beset by crime was Oklahoma, known during most of the frontier days as the Indian Territory, so called because of the five tribes (Cherokee, Creek, Seminole, Chickasaw, and Choctaw) sequestered there by the U.S. government. Although the conflict between Native Americans and white settlers was one of the most famous in the West, it was a challenge handled largely by the government and the military. Since routing them out was both dangerous and time consuming given the very little law enforcement available, outlaws made the area their headquarters. When the U.S. government opened the land to settlers in what would later be called the Oklahoma Land Rush, a whole new set of challenges arose in controlling the many disputes that developed over land rights. The skirmishes became the province of the western lawman.

On the streets of Dodge City, Kansas (pictured in 1878), many gunfighters earned reputations as very dangerous men.

As frontier expansion continued, other parts of the West became problem areas. The dispute over land rights also plagued parts of Wyoming and later New Mexico in what became bloody and bitter range wars. Sometimes the federal government was asked to step in to mediate but, not wanting to get involved in a local feud, the government often made this the jurisdiction of the local lawman.

The discovery of gold in California and silver in Nevada and Arizona created overnight boomtowns that became heavily populated in a short period of time. Mining law, which was based on judicial law but placed a greater emphasis on the miner's claim, was invoked until jurisdictions could be firmly established. Until that was accomplished, towns such as Tombstone, Arizona, were rife with such criminal activity as illegal gambling, prostitution, and liquor-induced violence.

Between Territory and Statehood

Criminal behavior was hard to control in part because legal jurisdictions were still evolving in territories without statehood. At first, the law of the land was the Northwest Ordinance, passed by Congress in 1787. As migration increased westward, county and city demarcations led to greater political organization. Eventually, territorial governors were appointed, county seats were established with presiding commissioners, and town councils were selected. The choice of a county seat, which benefited from prestige and government funding, sometimes became a violent battle in itself.

Each expansion of government created different levels of law enforcement. The highest level and one of the most legendary was that of U.S. marshal. Legislation enacted in 1789 held that a marshal was appointed by the president and approved by the Senate. The position did carry certain federal law enforcement responsibilities, but the job was largely bureaucratic. This left most of the tracking of wanted federal criminals in the hands of U.S. deputy marshals. These deputies were handpicked by the federal marshals, often based on records and reputations developed on the city and county level. The deputies did the dangerous work, but their loved ones shared the burden of danger. Zoe Tilghman, widow of Bill Tilghman, said, "He would shrug it off as just another job but a cold shiver would go up my spine when I saw him strap on his gun and look over his rifle. It was then I realized he was going after one or more men who would kill him rather than spend a good part of their lives behind bars."[4]

Sheriffs, who appointed their own deputies, were elected on the county level. A county sheriff's jurisdiction varied in size depending on the territory. The seat of Ford County, Kansas, was Dodge

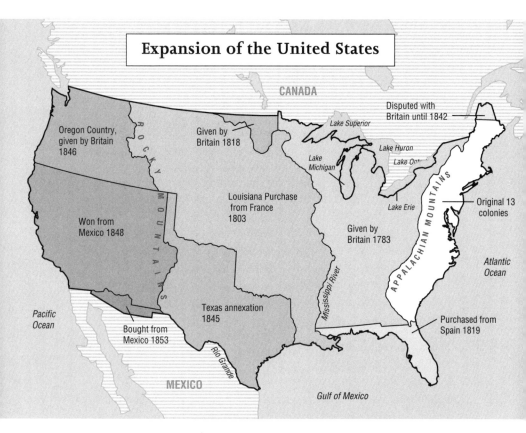

Expansion of the United States

CANADA

Oregon Country, given by Britain 1846

ROCKY MOUNTAINS

Given by Britain 1818

Lake Superior

Disputed with Britain until 1842

Lake Huron

Lake Michigan

Lake Ontario

Louisiana Purchase from France 1803

Won from Mexico 1848

Lake Erie

APPALACHIAN MOUNTAINS

Original 13 colonies

Given by Britain 1783

Atlantic Ocean

Pacific Ocean

Mississippi River

Texas annexation 1845

Bought from Mexico 1853

Rio Grande

Purchased from Spain 1819

MEXICO

Gulf of Mexico

City, making that jurisdiction one of the largest and most dangerous in the West. The deputies were charged with enforcement of local laws and the collection of taxes.

At the municipal level, a city council hired most local law enforcement officers. The council or mayor would hire the sheriff or marshal who, in turn, appointed their own undersheriffs and deputies with council approval. This staff, much like that of a county sheriff, rarely numbered more than four or five men in total. Responsibilities ranged from keeping the peace to cleaning the streets.

Other law enforcement organizations that existed in the Old West included the Texas Rangers, the model for current state police departments. The most famous private detective agency in the West was the Pinkerton Detective Agency, founded by Scottish immigrant Allan Pinkerton and nationally known for its agents' dogged determination. On Native American reservations, the U.S. government allowed Indians to police their own communities. However, if a crime was committed on the reservation by an outsider, or if a Native American committed a crime against a non-Native American, federal or local authorities took over.

The Toughest of the Tough

Life on the frontier was rugged, and some professions were more rugged than others. Cowboys and buffalo hunters, for example, had to endure all manner of natural and man-made conditions. This made their work extremely difficult, and it is no accident that although the lawmen of the West came from all walks of life, an inordinate amount initially worked as cowboys or buffalo hunters, or both.

In essence, if westerners had to be tough, then lawmen were the toughest of the tough—and legendary lawmen, a breed apart. Western historian Lee A. Silva wrote:

> This special breed of lawmen was made up of men who were not only the toughest of the tough, they were men who HAD TO BE the toughest of the tough—, for those who weren't were fated to end up in Boot Hill [dead], or if they lived long enough, be run out of town when their manly flaws were soon ferreted out by the human renegades who lived merely to test the mettle of another man.[5]

These men did this dangerous work for meager pay, which begs the question: Why would they undertake it at all? Some, such as Wyatt Earp, Bat Masterson, and Pat Garrett, became lawmen based on the circumstances they found themselves in. Others came to the profession for a variety of reasons, and often as not, it was a matter of pride.

If being a lawman meant being the toughest of the tough, then nothing could be tougher than being a lawman who refused to carry a gun. "Bear River" Tom Smith was one such man. The former New York City policeman earned his name for settling a mob riot in Bear River City, Wyoming. He was made marshal of Abilene, Texas, in June 1870 and did his job without ever wearing a gun. He succeeded for a time by simply outsmarting his opponents, but on November 2, 1870, a fugitive with an ax caught him off-guard and split his head open.

Smith's replacement in Abilene, the legendary Wild Bill Hickok, whose pride lay in his astounding ability with a gun, could not have possibly been more different from his predecessor. Hickok later quit the job after he accidentally shot his own deputy.

Between such extreme examples as Smith, who never used a gun, and Hickok, who always did, were lawmen like Marshal Willie Kennard, who had both Hickok's prowess with a gun and Smith's unerring ability to judge human behavior. In the gold-mining town of Yankee Hill, Colorado, in 1874, Kennard arrived to apply for the job of marshal. The forty-two-year-old black Civil War veteran was not taken seriously by the town council. As a joke, Mayor

While serving as a marshal in Abilene, Texas, Wild Bill Hickok was known for his ability with a gun.

Matt Borden told Kennard that if he wanted the job he would have to prove himself worthy by arresting Barney Casewit. Kennard did not know that Casewit was the reason the position of marshal was available; he had either killed or run out of town all the previous marshals. Casewit had also raped a fifteen-year-old girl and killed her father. Mayor Borden could not have found a more ruthless man to pit Kennard against. Kennard took up the challenge.

Kennard proved his mettle—and then some. He went to the local saloon to confront Casewit, who, like the town council, laughed off the gangly middle-aged man's request to come along quietly. Realizing Kennard was serious, Casewit reached for his holstered guns. Witnesses were amazed when Kennard shot the guns from Casewit's hands and then killed two of Casewit's nearby accomplices, who had their guns drawn and ready to fire. Casewit was taken into custody and Yankee Hill had a new marshal.

For the next two years, Kennard successfully tangled with other equally dangerous men. When a series of stagecoach robberies plagued the town, the known culprit proved impossible to flush out of the hills above Yankee Hill. Kennard placed wanted posters around town offering a mere fifty dollars for the capture of Billy McGeorge. Irate and insulted, McGeorge came out of the hills and was arrested by Kennard on sight. Despite these successes, Kennard left Yankee Hill in 1877, never to be heard from again.

The reasons men became lawmen are as varied as the men themselves. Whether it was a matter of pride or the need to prove themselves in adverse situations, these men were an important part of one of the most tumultuous times in U.S. history. Mostly forgotten now, the majority of western lawmen did their job without fanfare or great financial compensation. According to legendary lawman Bat Masterson, they were "just plain ordinary men who could shoot straight and had the most utter courage and perfect nerve—and for the most part, a keen sense of right and wrong."[6]

CHAPTER 2

Isaac Parker: The Hanging Judge

Not everyone who fought lawlessness in the Wild West wore a badge and carried a gun. Isaac Charles Parker did as much to clean up the West as any sheriff or marshal, but he did so without ever firing a single shot. Responsible for the deaths of almost eighty men, Parker's weapon of choice was a gavel. As the federal judge presiding over the vast Indian Territory that now makes up much of Oklahoma, Parker was vilified by some for his hard line on crime. Others, including current Supreme Court Chief Justice William Rehnquist, consider Parker one of the most influential jurists in U.S. history. Either way, Parker remains one of the most important figures of the Old West.

The Roots of Justice

If ancestry and upbringing can affect an individual's destiny, then such was the case with Isaac Parker. He was born the youngest son of Jane and Joseph Parker on October 15, 1838, in Barnesville, Ohio. He grew up on his parents' farm, but his heritage included six maternal great-uncles who pursued legal careers and public office. His mother's youngest uncle, Wilson Shannon, was elected the first native-born governor of the state.

Young Isaac grew up in southeastern Ohio when it was still largely agricultural and just barely out of the frontier stage. His parents, especially his mother, administered a strict Methodist upbringing, teaching him that the difference between right and wrong was primarily a matter of good and evil. This would greatly influence his legal career.

When not in school, Isaac was hard pressed to do his share of chores on the Parker farm. When he did do the work required of him, Isaac often carried his books with him and read whenever there was a break in his labors. Years later, his nephew said of Isaac, "It was hard to shame him to where he would clasp a pitchfork handle. [He was] always a hand to get an education."[7]

After completing Breeze Hill Primary School, Isaac chose to advance his education at the private Barnesville Classical Institute. Isaac paid the costly tuition with the salary he earned teaching younger students at a rural primary school. At the institute he earned a reputation as a fierce debater. Upon graduation, at the age of seventeen, he decided on a career in law.

Like most law students at the time, Parker combined apprenticeship and self-study to get an education in law. Parker paid an attorney, who allowed the young law student to observe the legal process. Parker also read everything he could find on jurisprudence. It was a grueling schedule of long hours and self-discipline, but the young student reveled in it. Parker handily passed his bar exam in 1859 on the strength of his ability to sway juries with his oratory and his acute logic.

Now twenty-one, with an impressive two hundred-pound, six-foot frame, Parker set his intense blue eyes on practicing law west of Ohio, preferably in Missouri, where he could look up family members who practiced law. He boarded a steamboat for the bustling port city of St. Joseph with the hope of finding employment in the law firm of his great-uncle, D.E. Shannon. In 1860 Parker was accepted as a partner in the St. Joseph law firm that was renamed Branch, Shannon and Parker.

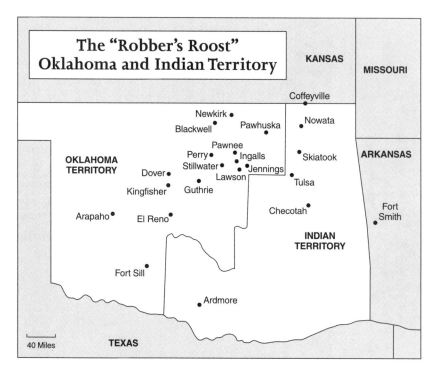

Love, War, and Politics

The next several years were eventful ones for Parker. He left the firm and gained trial experience on his own as a defense attorney. He used his considerable oratorical skill to sway local dignitaries, and had ambitions of political office. He also courted Mary O'-Toole, a local resident. He was elected city attorney on April 1, 1861, and on December 12 he and Mary were married.

The Civil War began just four days after the election. Parker enlisted in the 61st Missouri Emergency Regiment, a home guard unit. Parker had been elected city attorney as a Democrat, but as the war intensified, he reevaluated his beliefs and left the Democratic Party. By 1864 he was a substantial member of the Republican Party, helping elect Abraham Lincoln to a second term. Such political connections found Parker himself elected to higher office, first as county prosecutor and then as district judge. In 1870 a faction of the Republican Party convinced Parker to make a run for the House of Representatives. When his opponent dropped out two weeks before the election, Parker easily beat the replacement candidate.

As a freshman member of Congress, Parker sponsored legislation that, if passed, would have allowed women to vote and hold public office. He later earned national recognition for helping create the Bureau of Indian Affairs and organizing the Indian Territories. He was so successful with legislation for his own district that a local newspaper said of him, "Missouri had no more trusted or influential representative."[8]

After two terms in Congress, Parker sought a political appointment. President Ulysses S. Grant offered him a state supreme court judgeship in the Utah territory, but since he had been involved in the reorganization of the Indian Territory, Parker preferred an appointment to that district. On March 18, 1875, Grant formally nominated Parker to the district he had requested. Isaac C. Parker was

Isaac Parker served as a soldier in the Civil War before moving on to a successful career in politics and law.

confirmed as the federal judge of the Western District of Arkansas comprising the Indian Territory.

"Robber's Roost"

Parker had jurisdiction over seventy-four thousand square miles, stretching from the western edge of the Arkansas border to what is now Oklahoma and the southeastern edge of Colorado. This federal district, established by Congress in 1851 to preside over all crimes committed there (except for those by Native Americans against Native Americans), had been troublesome long before Parker arrived. It had been besieged by western expansion, cattle drives, the coming of the railroads, the Civil War, and the exile of Native Americans by treaty. These events, as well as the lack of proper law enforcement, made the area the perfect haven for the criminal element seeking refuge from the law. Newspapers had taken to calling it "Robber's Roost" for the number of wanted outlaws who operated openly in the area.

Attempts to bring any form of permanent justice to the region, and to the West in general, proved problematic. Judges and jurors were threatened with violence, courtrooms often saw rowdy brawls break out, and if a trial did go smoothly, there was the issue of making jurors aware of legal terminology. Author Mark Twain observed one juror who "thought that arson and incest were the same thing."[9]

When Parker arrived at the federal courthouse in Fort Smith, Arkansas, all of his considerable knowledge of and experience in the judicial system were brought to bear. Parker's predecessor, Judge William Story, had been caught up in a bribery scandal that might have led to his conviction had he not retired and fled the territory. Congress aided Parker with statutes for the district that mandated the sentence for all capital crime convictions (murder and rape): death. They also allowed Parker to be the judge of any appeals to his own court. Armed with these statutes, it was the new judge's responsibility to clean up a judicial system rife with corruption and criminal activity. Parker wasted no time addressing these issues.

Judge Parker Takes Over

Parker's first term as judge began on May 10, 1875, at age thirty-six and he remains one of the youngest federal judges in U.S. history. Congress had stipulated that court sessions run in four separate terms each year. Parker's caseload was so large, however, that the four terms ran together and he held court six days a week, often up to ten hours each day.

During those first sessions, Parker laid down the law as no other jurist in Indian Territory had done before him, and he continued to do so for the next two decades. Parker sentenced the first six men found guilty of murder to death by hanging. Three of the convicted men had killed their victims for petty larceny, while another had killed a man and his wife over a simple insult. The most heinous of the convicted proved to be a hardened killer who had made an officer of the law his eighth victim. Parker rendered his sentence in a lengthy declaration to the condemned in open court, which he concluded in a low voice, saying, "I do not desire to hang you men. It is the law."[10]

Parker scheduled all six men to be publicly executed at the same time, an unprecedented move meant to show the seriousness of

Pictured is the federal courthouse in Fort Smith, Arkansas, where Judge Parker held court six days a week.

their crimes and the court's seriousness in rendering justice. Citizens showed up en masse as newspapers from around the country covered the story. The men were executed on the gallows on September 3, 1875, with the local paper heralding, "Large Crowd—6 Murderers Hanged—Details of the Execution—Brief Sketches of Convicts and the Crimes for Which They Suffered." A national newspaper ran this condemning headline: "Cool Destruction of Six Human Lives by Legal Process."[11] This was the start of a conflict between Parker and those outside of the Indian Territory who disapproved of his tactics that would last until the end of his career.

What Parker's critics disapproved of was the harshness with which he meted out judicial due process to those brought before the court. The process began by the filing of a criminal complaint; then an arrest warrant was issued for Parker's deputies to bring in the accused. Pleas of not guilty went before Parker and the grand jury, which either dismissed or indicted, based on evidence. Indictments were called a true bill and resulted in a jury trial, with Parker issuing the sentence in the event of conviction. Murder and rape convictions carried a death sentence. Lesser crimes resulted in fines or prison terms, with terms longer than a year served in facilities back east.

Parker's Men

Previous, undisciplined courts had a difficult time with the judicial proceeding known as due process. Parker went to great lengths to ensure it was carried out, including giving very detailed jury instructions that often lasted up to two hours. He was concerned that the jurors understand both the crime and their own responsibility as jurors. Newspapers that felt he was leading the jury criticized Parker. He felt it justified, stating, "I tell you a jury should be led! If they are guided they will render justice."[12]

The most difficult part of the process was bringing the accused into custody. Parker did not create this standard process, nor did he carry out that aspect of the law. That most dangerous responsibility belonged to deputy marshals aptly described as "the Men Who Rode for Parker."[13] The pay was meager—two dollars for an arrest and six cents a mile for traveling—and the work was extremely perilous. During Parker's time on the bench, sixty-five of these men were killed in the line of duty. Parker was keenly aware of the danger these men faced, and, unlike previous judges, freely raised the issue in court if it figured into the trial of the accused. He made sure to always pay them their due, saying, "Without these officers, what is the use of this court?"[14]

Judge Parker's deputy marshals did the dangerous work of bringing lawbreakers before the bench. Many of these men died in the line of duty.

The deputies came under the jurisdiction of the U.S. marshal, but it is not fully known who hired them. Most were white, but they were of diverse backgrounds, and some had shady records. In some cases, Parker was directly involved in selection; he apparently favored Native Americans and African Americans, who could freely enter Indian Territory without raising suspicion, since they had been welcomed there during the Civil War. Parker's choices created one of the most integrated law enforcement communities in the West.

Condemned men encountered another member of Parker's court, George Maledon. Tall, bearded, and somber, Maledon was Fort Smith's executioner for twenty-two years. Maledon executed sixty men on the gallows, more men than any other modern executioner. His unsentimental assessment of his competence was "I never hanged a man who came back to have the job done over."[15]

Parker's Court

A working federal court now firmly established, Parker also managed to work hard on civic improvements to Fort Smith and the

Indian Territory. Having brought Mary and his two young sons from Missouri shortly after his own arrival, Parker became a very active member of the school board and worked for criminal reform, Native American improvement, and other civic causes. Out of court, the citizens of Fort Smith knew him to be affable and approachable. Many were surprised to see him walk to and from court each day, well aware that he had made enemies who made no secret of their hatred of him and their desire for vengeance.

Most of his time was spent in court hearings, his docket ranging from simple assault cases to sensational murder trials. The mandatory death sentences he handed down gave rise to closer scrutiny by newspapers and, eventually, by Congress.

During his term on the bench, Parker ordered the execution of more than eighty men. The most notorious case brought an end to the careers of the ruthless Rufus Buck Gang. Buck and his four henchmen went on a two-week crime spree that resulted in two deaths and two rapes. When they were finally apprehended, Parker saw them successfully tried for murder, then had the

The members of the Rufus Buck Gang are the only outlaws in American history to have been sentenced to death for rape.

defendants keep their seats while a new jury entered for the rape trial. Found guilty on all charges, the Buck Gang are the only men in U.S. history to be sentenced to death for rape.

Congress Steps In

Three men Parker condemned to the gallows in 1881 had unsuccessfully pleaded self-defense during their trials. Parker often advised juries to ignore claims of self-defense, which brought his courtroom procedure under closer scrutiny by Congress. Public opinion, fanned by newspapers outside his jurisdiction, brought accusations of heartlessness and brutality against Parker. For his part, Parker stood by his record: "People . . . have called me a heartless man, a bloodthirsty man, but no one has pointed to a specific case of undue severity. They are given to say 'Judge Parker is too rigid' but they do not point to any one case."[16]

Parker was criticized for other tactics in his courtroom. His lengthy rulings (sometimes lasting several hours) were attacked as being extremely biased. When he sentenced one infamous outlaw, Parker ended with this statement:

> The crime you have committed is but another evidence, if any were needed, of your wicked, lawless, bloody and murderous disposition. It is another evidence of your total disregard of human life; another evidence that you revel in the destruction of human life. The many murders you have committed, and their reckless and wanton character, show you to be a human monster from whom innocent people can expect no safety.[17]

In 1889 Congress acted to relieve Parker of some of his power. First, legislators reassigned some of his jurisdiction to two other federal court districts, and then, in the same year, they stopped Parker from hearing appeals to his own court. This allowed the Supreme Court to hear appeals from prisoners Parker had sentenced. The series of events that followed would mold the modern appellate system and bring an end to Parker's reign as a justice in the Old West.

Judge Parker Versus the Supreme Court

The Supreme Court did not hear appeals from Parker's court immediately, since it was difficult to find a defense attorney brave enough to challenge the judge's ruling. Lawyers were easily intimidated by Parker and, as one deputy marshal noted, "When an attorney started to argue with him, he just a pointed his finger at him. The attorney didn't sit down, he fell down."[18]

One lawyer was brave enough to accept the challenge: a flamboyant attorney named J. Walter Reed. He took full advantage of the appeal process and petitioned the Supreme Court many times. The Court struck down Parker's rulings on grounds ranging from inappropriate jury instructions to the exclusion of self-defense pleas. Of the forty-six appeals brought before them from Parker's jurisdiction, the Court overturned the trial judge thirty times. Parker thought these rulings were based on technicalities and took the appeals personally, saying, "The appellate court exists mainly to stab the trial judge in the back . . . and enable the criminal to go free."[19]

The End of the Federal Court

Parker's battle with the Supreme Court occurred during a tumultuous time in that part of the West. In 1889 the federal government released large tracts of land in the Indian Territory to anyone who staked a claim to them. During this time, known as the Oklahoma Land Rush, people swarmed into the area for a chance to own land, swelling the population. Congress found it necessary to chip away further at Parker's jurisdiction, with even more redistricting legislated in 1895. This brought an end to Parker's reign over the federal court in the Western District of Arkansas.

Judge Parker's reputation for tough sentences and for hearing his own appeals forced Congress to limit his power.

Parker fell ill from a combination of ailments and retired from the bench. By the time he retired, he had presided over 13,490 cases, of which 9,454 resulted in guilty verdicts. He spent his remaining days going for walks with Mary and giving interviews to the local paper from his sickbed. Looking back over his career, he said, "I have ever had the single aim of justice in view. . . . 'Do equal and exact justice,' is my motto, and I have often said to the grand jury, 'Permit no innocent man to be punished, but let no guilty man escape.' . . . We are proud of the record of the court at Ft. Smith. We believe we have checked a flood of crime."[20]

In his absence, Parker's court convened once more on September 1, 1896. Judge Isaac Charles Parker died on November 17, 1896, at the age of fifty-eight. His death drew national attention and many dignitaries attended his funeral. Prisoners he had sentenced were reported to have rejoiced at the news, but some of his legal adversaries, including J. Walter Reed, mourned his passing.

Not all of Parker's adversaries were so kind. S.W. Harman, a defense attorney from Fort Smith, published a book two years after Parker's death entitled *Hell on the Border*, creating a much more vicious image of the jurist. Over time, others followed suit and the nickname "Hanging Judge" was permanently affixed to Parker in books, movies, and TV shows. Whether this image is accurate is still being debated, making the impact of Parker's attempt to bring law and order to the West one of the most controversial in American history.

CHAPTER 3

Wyatt Earp: Reluctant Legend

Wyatt Earp is arguably the most famous lawman of the Old West. However, his status as a legendary lawman is more the result of circumstance than of conscious effort. Earp did not avoid dangerous situations, but he did not seek them out. A man of good instincts, intelligence, and natural courage, Wyatt Earp became a lawman simply by virtue of the choices he made in a given situation. His early life molded him into a man capable of making those choices.

Early Lessons

Earp's father, Nicholas Earp, had fathered a son, Newton, with his first wife, Abigail. She died in 1839, and the following year Nicholas married Virginia Cooksey, who gave birth to the remaining Earp children. Wyatt Stapp Berry Earp was born March 19, 1848, in Monmouth, Illinois. His birth followed that of his brothers James and Virgil. Two daughters did not survive infancy, but the remaining Earp children, Morgan, Warren, and daughter Adelia (Addie), grew to adulthood.

Nicholas Earp, a farmer by trade, had always had a streak of wanderlust, and he moved his family often over the years if a chance for a better life seemed possible. As a youth, Wyatt lived in Iowa, Kentucky, and California. Often the new boy in a neighborhood as well as the middle of several brothers, Wyatt quickly learned how to take care of himself. He fought occasionally in school when he thought a smaller child was being bullied, and once even fought a grown man who whipped his horse too much for Wyatt's satisfaction. As was the custom of the time, Wyatt also was taught to use firearms at an early age, and his skill impressed his father and older brothers. "It is not conceit for me to say that I was the best shot in the family," Wyatt said years later. "Accuracy with firearms came naturally to me."[21]

As the Earps moved west and Wyatt and his brothers reached adulthood, they encountered many dangerous adventures, including attacks by Native Americans and the temporary loss of James and Virgil to the Civil War. Wyatt helped support his family however possible and managed to get work as a freight coach driver, traveling a route that stretched from Los Angeles to Salt Lake City. When he was seventeen he left home and sought out many more adventures on his own, always checking in with his family throughout the years.

It was while he was visiting his family in Lamar, Missouri, that he first found work as a lawman. His father, who was the justice of the peace, secured his son a job as constable. Earp enjoyed the work and began courting a young woman named Urilla Sutherland. They married in 1870, but the next year, pregnant with their child, Urilla succumbed to an outbreak of typhoid. Earp was so devastated by the loss that he left Lamar, and no record exists of him ever officially marrying again, though he did have relationships with other women.

Drifting with the Buffalo

Over the next several years, Earp dabbled in different occupations until he found what suited him best. He and older brother Virgil found buffalo hunting to be a lucrative undertaking and proceeded to make a profitable venture of it. Earp used his ingenuity to improve upon the method of hunting by sneaking up to a herd and firing from a standing position in contrast to the popular method of riding into a herd and firing at full gallop. Earp's method prevented the buffalo from stampeding, allowing him to kill the largest and most powerful of the herd. He also enjoyed the camaraderie of other hunters in the camps that were set up to follow the flow of the herd. One such hunter, Bat Masterson, would remain a lifelong friend.

During his buffalo hunting days, Earp caught two gamblers playing crooked poker in one of the makeshift camps. He observed their game for some time and then stepped in to play. When he caught them cheating, Earp told them to put down their cards and not reach for anything else. Before they could react, Earp held up his cards in his left hand and pointed his gun at them with his right, getting the gamblers to quietly leave the camp. When asked later why he did not shoot the men but only made them leave, Earp said, "That was all the occasion called for."[22]

When buffalo hunting was slow, Wyatt and Virgil worked for the railroads. In Wyoming they got into a fistfight with three much larger men who had been taunting them. Virgil held his own but eventually lost, while Wyatt lasted only about a half minute

Pictured from left are the Earp brothers, Wyatt, Virgil, and Morgan, participants in the famous 1881 gunfight in Tombstone, Arizona.

before taking a pummeling from a man known as "Big Swede." He decided to take boxing lessons the very next day from a professional and learned all the rules to proper fighting, even refereeing a few fights in the railroad camp. His sister Addie recalled that "one of the last things Wyatt did before leaving the railroad job was to call on that Big Swede. Wyatt mauled him bad and was pretty pleased."[23]

By 1872 Earp had drifted into Kansas, where the most important phase of his life would be initiated. It began with his courting Celia Blaylock, known as Mattie to her friends, and in time she became his common-law wife. The union was troubled from the start, with Mattie maintaining an increasing dependency on the narcotic laudanum, which would eventually end her life.

Hell Is in Session

It was in the town of Ellsworth that Earp's legend began to build. Ellsworth was a Kansas cow town that was quickly gaining a reputation for criminal activity. It escalated to the point that the Kansas State News ran the headline: "As we go to press, Hell is in session in Ellsworth."[24]

In August 1873 Earp was in Ellsworth gambling in a local saloon. Famed Texas gunfighter Ben Thompson and his younger brother Billy had been removed from the saloon by Sheriff Chauncey B. Whitney for causing a disturbance with another gambler. As they crossed the street, Billy Thompson shot and killed the sheriff. Ben convinced his brother to leave town while he gathered other Texas cowboys to join him in protecting his brother's exit so a posse would not be formed. For more than an hour Thompson stood armed with a shotgun and six-shooter in front of a hotel in the middle of town taunting townsfolk in an attempt to keep them from going after his brother.

When Mayor Jim Miller discovered that no lawman was willing to confront the famous gunfighter, he promptly fired them all. Earp had witnessed the event, and told the mayor that if it were his business he would take Ben Thompson in. The mayor took the badge of one of the deputies he had fired and pinned it on Earp. Earp went to a nearby store, bought a pair of used guns, and crossed the street to face Thompson. As he did, he saw Thompson's armed men strategically placed around him. Earp engaged Thompson in conversation as he got closer, to keep the men from firing their weapons. He later said, "I knew what I would do before the mayor pinned the badge on my shirt. I based my action on the knowledge of Ben Thompson's vanity and the Texas men in the crowd."[25]

In Ellsworth, Kansas (pictured in 1867), Wyatt Earp forced reputed gunfighter Ben Thompson to surrender his guns without firing a shot.

Earp got Thompson to surrender his guns and go to jail without ever firing a shot as Thompson's men held their fire during the conversation. Thompson later said he genuinely believed Earp would have shot him if he went for his guns. For Earp's part, he later admitted that he fully expected to be killed, saying, "That's the chance any officer has to take and for the time being I was taking the place of an officer. . . . I couldn't bear to see him get away with what he was doing. People have a right to live in peace and he was protecting the getaway of his brother who for pure meanness had killed a good man."[26]

Wichita, Kansas

Miller offered Earp a permanent job as a deputy, but he declined. He continued to drift and much of his whereabouts during this time remains unaccounted for. In 1874 he was in Wichita visiting his brother James when another event forced him to take action. As Earp was checking into the hotel, he saw hotel

As a deputy marshal in Wichita, Kansas, Wyatt Earp kept the peace for two years before moving on to Dodge City.

owner Doc Black beating a sixteen-year-old boy. Earp came to the boy's defense, beat up Black, and was promptly arrested. By this time the story involving Ben Thompson had spread and the town sheriff and mayor visited Earp in jail. They offered Earp a job as deputy marshal, telling him that the Thompson story must be true since Doc Black was the biggest bully in town and had never been bested. This time Earp accepted the offer.

As a deputy marshal in Wichita, Earp's job was fairly routine for most of the year. The exception was when the cowboys rode into town at the end of the trail. Earp and the other lawmen had to keep the peace while maintaining the cowboy presence that brought economic stability to the town. This often proved difficult, as in the case of Shanghai Pierce. Pierce was a big man, physically and financially, and when the drunken 240-pound Texas cattle baron refused to heed Earp's request to give up his guns, a near riot ensued. As Pierce and the other Texas cowboys chased Earp, the wily deputy eluded them through town before sneaking behind Pierce and holding him at gunpoint until the cowboys gave up their guns. As they were escorted out of town, Ben Thompson, who was staying at a local hotel, shouted down to Pierce, "I told you Wyatt Earp was poison."[27]

On another occasion Earp chose to take the law into his own hands when a local citizen refused to stop taunting him about the Thompson incident. George Peshaur harangued Earp regularly, claiming that Earp was not physically capable of taking on the infamous Ben Thompson. Finally, Earp volunteered to take off his guns and meet with Peshaur in the back room of Dick Cogswell's cigar store. The much larger Peshaur agreed, and over the next several minutes the sound of crashing furniture could be heard throughout the town. When it was over, Cogswell said, "I don't think there was a square inch of [Peshaur's] face that wasn't raw as beefsteak."[28]

After the lawlessness of Wichita was quelled, Earp's reputation earned him an invitation to bring order to Dodge City. The rowdiness of Ellsworth and Wichita paled in comparison to Dodge, where the cattle trails had shifted with the coming railroads. City officials offered Earp a generous $250 a month as deputy marshal. Under Marshal Larry Deger, Earp would be working with other noted deputies such as Bat Masterson, Bill Tilghman, and Charlie Bassett. He accepted their offer and went to Dodge in the spring of 1876.

The Queen of the Cow Towns

The Wyatt Earp who appeared in Dodge—known as "The Queen of the Cow Towns"—was the Earp of legend. Tall and slender, with a large, flowing mustache set beneath steel blue eyes, Earp strolled the streets of Dodge looking every inch the western lawman of American mythology. He wasted no time in helping to establish strict guidelines for law and order. The prohibition of firearms in town was strictly enforced along with other regulations that Earp and the rest of the deputies worked hard to maintain.

Aiding Earp's reputation was a specially made gun given to him by writer Ned Buntline, called the Buntline Special. It had an extra long barrel and a removable stock that allowed it to be fired as a rifle if needed. "Mine was my favorite over any other gun," Earp said. "I carried it at my right hip throughout my career."[29]

The presence of Wyatt Earp and his specially made firearm went a long way toward keeping the peace in Dodge. Earp's unique ap-

In 1876 Wyatt Earp became a deputy marhsal in Dodge City, where rowdy scenes like this were a frequent occurrence.

proach in dealing with adversaries also helped: Contrary to popular legend, Earp very rarely used his gun to shoot, choosing instead to "buffalo" his adversary. By this tactic, Earp would catch the man off guard and use the heavy butt of his gun to knock him unconscious. This highly successful method incapacitated an adversary without irrevocable, possibly controversial consequences.

Earp was involved in many of the legendary events of Dodge, but mostly in a supporting role to the other deputies. On a personal level, the most important event that arose from his tenure in Dodge was the unlikely friendship that developed between Earp and a sickly part-time dentist and full-time gambler named Doc Holliday. The bond between the Kansas lawman and the Georgia gambler would become of life-and-death importance to Earp and is one of the most written about friendships in history. According to Bat Masterson, "Doc had but three redeeming traits. One was his courage. The second was his sterling loyalty. The third was his affection for Wyatt Earp."[30]

Tombstone, Arizona

Wyatt Earp did not stay long in Dodge City once the rowdiness was brought under control. He and Mattie had moved on and by 1880 had settled in the mining boomtown of Tombstone, Arizona. There they had a family reunion of sorts with brothers Virgil, James, and Morgan, who had settled in Tombstone with their families. Wyatt believed he could finally hang up his guns and turn to other business interests, such as running a saloon or a profitable gambling house. This dream was short lived, as almost immediately the Earp brothers ran afoul of some the more unsavory locals. Wyatt also created tension at home by falling in love with an actress named Josie Marcus. It did not help that Doc Holliday had also drifted into Tombstone, bringing with him a deadly reputation for bloodshed as a gunfighter.

Tombstone had its own well-earned reputation for bloodshed. "The grimly humorous phrase about our town was that Tombstone had 'a man for breakfast every morning,' meaning someone was killed every night,"[31] said Josie Marcus. What transpired in Tombstone after the Earps arrived culminated the following year behind the O.K. Corral, in the most famous and hotly debated gunfight in the history of the American West.

Virgil had found work as a lawman but ran afoul of corrupt sheriff John Behan, believed to be a pawn of the horse-rustling Clanton and McLaury brothers and their cohorts, "Curly Bill" Brosches, Johnny Ringo, Pete Spence, Frank Stillwell, and a man called "Indian Charlie." The Clantons—Ike, Phinn, and Billy—resented the Earps' attempt to clean up the town to the extent that Virgil deputized Morgan and Wyatt to help him outmaneuver Behan. Several encounters with the Clanton Gang eventually led to the events of the afternoon of October 26, 1881.

Doc Holliday

Wyatt's Vendetta

A showdown was inevitable and although he wanted to abandon his guns, Wyatt chose to stand by his brothers when they faced the Clantons and McLaurys. Doc Holliday joined the Earps as they walked down Tombstone's Allen Street to meet their foes. The gunfight was

Wyatt Earp relocated to Tombstone, Arizona, in 1880, where he met up with his friend Doc Holliday (at left).

short, over in thirty seconds by some accounts, but when the smoke cleared, the McLaurys and most of the Clantons lay mortally wounded. Virgil, Morgan, and Doc had also been shot. Only Wyatt Earp and Ike Clanton stood unscathed.

This tumultuous event did not end the feud between the two warring factions. There was a trial in which the Earps were exonerated, but the following year an unseen gunman fired a crippling shot at Virgil. Later, Morgan was shot and died in Wyatt's arms after a bullet cracked through the window of the saloon they were in.

Wyatt Earp, believing his family honor was more important than obeying the law, gathered a posse consisting of Doc Holliday and several others. One by one they hunted down all the remaining members of the Clanton gang. When this was accomplished to Earp's satisfaction, he and Josie left Tombstone with a warrant for murder on his head, and he never looked back. He would later say, "For my handling of the situation at Tombstone, I have no regrets. Were it to be done again, I would do it exactly as I did it at the time."[32]

A Foul Blow

Josie and Wyatt's life together proved to be just as eventful after they left Tombstone. They traveled the West and even mined gold in Alaska for a time. Earp's old friend Bat Masterson had used his influence to get the charges against him dropped, allowing Wyatt and Josie to breathe easier as they traveled.

In 1896 Earp was involved in another controversy when he was asked to referee a championship boxing match between Jack Sharkey and Bob Fitzsimmons in San Francisco. Accusing Fitzsimmons of a foul blow, Earp gave the match to the near unconscious Sharkey. The decision created an embarrassing scandal, sending Earp and Josie south to finally settle in Los Angeles. In spite of such events, Josie considered their golden years together after Tombstone some of their best. She said, "Wyatt and I were discovering new things about each other each day. . . . One of the

In 1881 in a vacant lot near the O.K. Corral (pictured), the Earp brothers and Doc Holliday staged a shootout with the McLaury brothers and the Clanton family.

Near the end of his life, Earp (pictured in 1926) worked as a consultant on the set of western films.

first things we realized we had in common was an insatiable desire to travel, to see new people and places."[33]

At the end of his life, Earp worked as an advisor on westerns in the new medium of motion pictures. A writer named Stuart Lake collaborated with Earp on an autobiography, but Earp did not live to see it published. On January 23, 1929, at the age of eighty, Wyatt Earp died peacefully in his sleep. His autobiography, *Wyatt Earp, Frontier Marshal*, was a huge success, becoming the basis for the many portrayals of Wyatt Earp in the media over the next several decades. In the 1950s a popular TV show based on the book made Earp a favorite hero.

Over time, several errors in Lake's research were discovered, provoking a debate among historians and researchers over the veracity of Earp's accomplishments. More recently, new evidence has shown that Lake's errors were minor, and the record of Wyatt Earp has stood the test of time.

CHAPTER 4

Frank Canton: Alias Joe Horner

Renowned lawman Frank Canton started life as Joe Horner, a young Texas desperado whose vicious crimes included armed robbery and murder. He lived most of his adult life trying to bury his past by building an impressive career as a lawman throughout the West. Although not as well known as other figures, Canton was, according to Old West historian James D. Horan, "One of the most incredible figures in the wild west. . . . [who] left dead men and legends from Wyoming to the Klondike."[34]

He was born Josiah W. Horner on September 19, 1849, in Harrison, Indiana, the middle of nine children born to John and Mary Jane Horner. Their marriage produced four sons and five daughters, with almost every child born in a different state. The family constantly moved because John Horner, although limited in formal education, traveled widely working as a farmer, Methodist preacher, and even a doctor. Although they were constantly uprooted, John and Mary Jane went to great pains to ensure that their children were well provided for.

The mobility of the family aside, things remained fairly uneventful for the Horners until the Civil War. John Horner was a military surgeon for the Confederacy and eventually died in a Union prison camp. Although only fourteen, Joe Horner had run away and joined the Union as an orderly. After the war he drifted into Texas and found work as a cowboy. He was strong and powerfully built for his age, but also possessed a vicious temper.

Reckless Youth

Horner's descent into crime began with midnight raids across the border into Indian Territory to steal first horses and then cattle from the local tribes. He would then sell the cattle to the U.S. Army post at Fort Richardson in north Texas. These raids were intermittent and executed with the help of several accomplices, including Frank Lake, whom Horner had met in the nearby town of Jacksboro. The town was rowdy, with daily saloon brawls and racial tension running high because of the large number of black soldiers living at Fort Richardson.

On October 10, 1874, Horner's criminal activity quickly spiraled into even lower depths. Leaving Lake with the cattle at Fort Richardson, Horner went into Jacksboro to meet the military official who would pay him for the beef. In a foul mood over several warrants recently issued for his horse-stealing activities, Horner went into one of Jacksboro's many saloons. The one he chose was fairly crowded with people, including two black soldiers. Words passed before Horner shot one of the soldiers, Pvt. George Smith, and the other fled. It is not known exactly what prompted the shooting, but Smith survived. Meanwhile, Horner went to another saloon, where he met Frank Lake. When the cavalry came to arrest Horner, he opened fire on them. During the ensuing shootout, Horner killed another black soldier before making his escape.

Hiding out, Horner hired a lawyer to draw up a treaty that might appease the army. It stated, among other things: "Mr. Horner agrees not to kill anymore negroes if the negroes would

In this 1885 photo, masked gunmen approach a ranch in Nebraska in order to steal cattle. Joe Horner started as a cattle thief.

not kill anymore of him."[35] The army eventually dropped all criminal charges, handing down only a civil indictment for assault, which was added to the existing charges of horse theft and cattle rustling.

While in custody awaiting trial, Horner escaped on September 13, 1875. He and his gang began a crime spree that was trailed by Sheriff Henry Strong to the city of Comanche, where they tried to rob a bank. Strong saw them mount their horses and tell the bank employees, "Charge this to the James Boys!"[36] He organized a posse that used the bank's marked bills to catch each gang member individually, getting Horner in San Antonio.

Horner escaped to rob a stagecoach but was again caught on April 19, 1877. Sent to Huntsville Penitentiary in shackles and under armed guard, Horner thought long and hard about his future. He ultimately decided it would be best to court authority figures instead of bucking them. His fifteen-year prison sentence was well timed, since Texas had recently passed legislation that was more lenient toward prisoners. While working outside the prison, he escaped once more on August 4, 1879, and convicted outlaw Joe Horner was never heard from again.

Frank Canton, Wyoming Lawman

It is not known exactly why Horner chose the name Frank M. Canton; historians speculate that it is a combination of the names of his friend Frank Lake and the town of Canton, Texas. Frank Canton first made his presence known in the Wyoming cattle country in 1880. As he would do throughout his life, Canton made friends with many influential people in the area and was eventually hired as a stock inspector by the Wyoming Stock Growers Association (WSGA) on August 22, 1881.

WSGA secretary Thomas Sturgis hired Canton because of his impressive knowledge of cattle rustlers and outlaws, unaware how that knowledge was attained. Sturgis said of his new employee: "In manners he was exceedingly quiet and unassuming, with a low, distinct voice that [was] never heard raised above an ordinary conversational tone. There was no limit however to his nerve, even if his ways were modest."[37]

Canton proved so successful and well liked in the job as stock inspector that he was elected sheriff of Johnson County in 1882, at a salary of $250 a month. In his first two years on the job, Canton ended the rash of horse rustling that had plagued the county. Thirteen of the sixteen men Canton sent to prison were convicted of horse stealing. By 1883 he could add U.S. deputy marshal to his

Frank Canton was appointed the sheriff of Johnson County, Wyoming, in part because of his experiences as a cattle thief.

resume. Things were going so well for him that in January 1885, Canton married the teenaged Annie Wilkerson, and in December she gave birth to their daughter, Ruby. Another daughter died shortly after infancy.

Canton's most famous arrest was that of a notorious horse thief known as Teton Jackson. The capture was based on a tip from a WSGA detective. Canton and two of his deputies quietly approached Jackson's cabin and got the drop on him and several of his gang members. Canton held Jackson at gunpoint while the deputies rounded up the stolen horses. Jackson later wrote Canton from prison requesting money for tobacco. Canton sent him a twenty-dollar bill, part of the reward money he had earned for capturing Jackson.

During his tenure as sheriff, Canton took note of a frustrating trend. Many of the rustlers in the area were migrant settlers from Europe desperate to eke out a living. Although Canton captured many cattle rustlers, juries tended to look the other way when thieves stole cattle from the big ranch owners. This frustration led Canton to leave the office of sheriff and become a stock detective for the WSGA in January 1887. As a stock detective, he was more closely involved in helping the big ranchers apprehend rustlers. This gave Canton greater satisfaction in stemming the tide of cattle rustling and also quenched his need to be near the influence of power. These factors would culminate in one of the most controversial events in the history of the American West.

The Johnson County War

By 1892 the rustling of cattle had reached epidemic proportions. The WSGA agreed to take drastic measures and hired up to fifty gunmen to enter the rustlers' territory in an attempt to end the epidemic. Led by former army officer Major Frank Wolcott, with Canton second in command and armed with a death list of names, the small army left the train depot on horseback and made their way up to Powder River. One of the names topping the list was

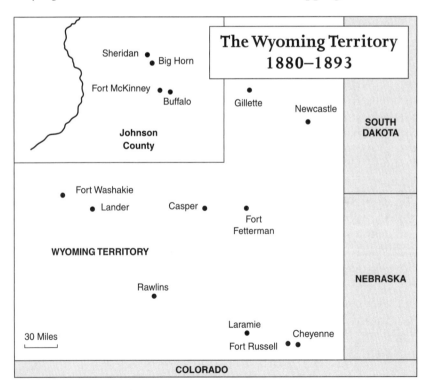

Nate Champion, an excellent marksman who sided with the rustlers. Canton and several other men had failed in their attempt to kill Champion months earlier, making him the most important target on their list.

On the morning of April 5, in the midst of a freezing snowstorm, the gunmen surrounded Champion's cabin. They had severely underestimated Champion, who had barricaded himself and several others in the small dwelling and succeeded in holding off the gunmen most of the day. While inside, Champion also managed to keep a journal of the events and noted every move his opposition made. His last entry read, "I heard them splitting wood. I guess they are going to fire the house tonight. I think I will make a break when night comes, if alive. Shooting again. It's not night yet. The house is all fired. Goodbye boys, if I never see you again. Nate Champion."[38]

The fire Champion wrote about was the result of Canton's idea to ignite a buckboard, a type of small wagon, and send it careening into the cabin. With his cohorts dead, Champion bolted from the burning cabin with his guns blazing. The gunmen riddled him with bullets and, as he lay in a heap, Frank Canton removed the blood-soaked diary from Champion's vest pocket.

The Johnson County War, as it came to be known, waged on, but Canton was dramatically affected by these events. He gave Champion's diary to the local newspaper, which printed it, severely altering public opinion concerning the WSGA. As much as Canton tried to remain professional, he was devastated by the range war in which he was immersed. By some accounts, Canton was haunted with dreams and often woke up shouting, "Do you hear them? They're coming! Get to your guns boys!"[39] In early 1894 Frank Canton and his family left Wyoming and tried to put the recent events of his life behind him.

Oklahoma Territory

Canton decided to ply his trade as a lawman in the Oklahoma Territory. A major factor in his decision involved a friend from his past. His former partner in crime, Frank Lake, had become a sheriff in the new town of Pawnee, and Lake was unable to stem the tide of outlaws when his request for martial law was denied by the government. Instead, he got the aid of his old friend Joe Horner, now living as Frank Canton. Canton chose to help his old friend, this time on the side of the law as an appointed undersheriff. Over the next two years, Canton, Lake, and their deputies ended much of the horse thievery and cattle rustling in the area. On one occasion,

Canton even sent another burning buckboard into a cabin to successfully dislodge two rustlers.

Canton had another motive in choosing Oklahoma. Because the territory bordered Texas, he took the opportunity to try to do something about his shady past. In his usual manner when dealing with powerful people, Canton approached Governor James S. Hogg of Texas about a full pardon. Over a short period of time he courted the governor's favor until he was able to make a personal appointment to officially request a pardon. In July 1894, fifteen years after his prison escape as Joe Horner, Canton's request was honored. The official language granted "to said convict Joe Horner a full, unconditional pardon in each case, restoring to him all his rights of citizenship and the right of suffrage [his right to vote]."[40] Knowing that his past might still endanger his job, Canton kept the pardon as secret as possible.

Now that his pardon was secured, Canton set his sights on capturing the Bill Doolin Gang, the most wanted outlaws in the territory. In March 1895, against his better judgement, Canton went along with Lake in signing an agreement with the notorious Dunn brothers. The five brothers, headed by Bee Dunn, agreed that if all previous charges of cattle rustling against them were dropped, they would give the lawmen information to help them find the Doolin Gang. Months passed without a word from the Dunns while other lawmen caught or killed members of the Doolin Gang, including Bill Doolin.

Canton, furious over the way things transpired, waged a massive campaign against Bee Dunn. He reinstated the cattle rustling charges against Dunn and arrested the man who processed Dunn's stolen cattle. Canton then told a newspaper he believed Bee Dunn, not Marshal Heck Thomas, shot and killed Bill Doolin. Canton knew this accusation would tarnish Dunn's reputation among other outlaws. Infuriated, Dunn vowed to get Canton, setting the stage for a violent confrontation. Canton was entering a local store when Dunn stood on the steps inside the building and shouted: "Damn you Canton, I've got it in for you!"[41] His gun caught for an instant on his suspenders, allowing Canton to draw his own gun and fire a single shot into Dunn's forehead, killing him instantly.

Alaskan Marshal

Canton's restlessness set in again following the killing of Bee Dunn. The political climate had changed, and he worried that his new supervisors would uncover his criminal record while evaluating his performance. He began to drink heavily and ex-

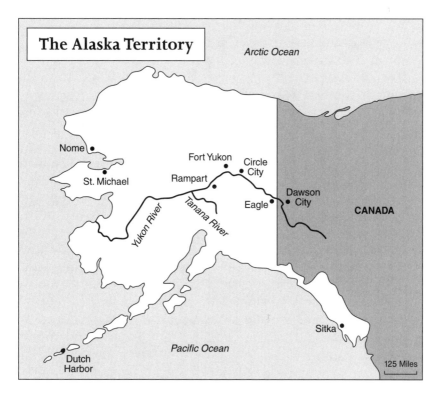

The Alaska Territory

Arctic Ocean

Nome

Fort Yukon
Circle
City
St. Michael
Rampart
Dawson
Eagle
City
CANADA

Sitka

Pacific Ocean

Dutch
Harbor

125 Miles

hibited uncharacteristic behavior. U.S. Deputy Marshal Charles Colcord, Canton's friend and coworker, was mystified by Canton's reaction to news of the death of Marshal George Horner, unaware that the two men were brothers. Later, after learning the truth, Colcord reflected, "During all the years I had known Frank I had never seen tears in his eyes, but they were there when Horner died."[42] Shortly after the death of his brother, Canton decided to go to Alaska.

Klondike fever was the reason given for anyone choosing to rough it in the wilds of Alaska after gold was discovered. Canton figured he could underwrite his prospecting activities with a federal marshal appointment to Alaska. The appointment was very slow in coming as Canton, now approaching fifty, left wife and daughter with his family in Wyoming and slogged through the Klondike, a region in eastern Alaska. Canton was destitute when his appointment finally came through, ordering him to make his way up a frozen river to an area in Woodworth dubbed "Suckerville." When he got there he found out why. Several outlaws had taken over the area of an abandoned ship when their gold prospecting did not pan out. These desperate men wreaked havoc on the innocent inhabitants of the ship who were also stranded there.

Winter had set in, leaving Canton and the others no choice but to wait until the thaw came. Canton recognized the outlaw ringleader as Tom Barkley, a wanted man in Idaho whom Canton never let out of his sight, in hopes of collecting the reward. When the thaw did come it was dramatic, as mighty chunks of ice crashed into the river. Canton was awestruck by the way Barkley risked his life to save a woman stranded on an ice floe. This so impressed Canton he did something he had never done before, and never did again. "I let $3,500 slip through my hands when I turned him loose and sent him down the Yukon River,"[43] Canton said.

Canton continued to work alone in the area of Circle City, with intermittent help from the military. The outlaws he brought in were housed and cared for by Canton without government reimbursement. In the summer of 1899, Canton was struck with snow-blindness and decided to return home once his eyesight improved.

The State of Oklahoma

It took quite a while for Canton's pay to finally reach him after he returned home in 1900. In the interim, Canton spent time in Wyoming working and reuniting with his wife and daughter. Although still waiting for his Alaskan pay, he could not get work as a lawman because of rumors of financial wrongdoing while in Alaska. He spent the next several years working alternately as a bounty hunter, city deputy, deputy marshal, and stock detective in many of his old haunts throughout the West. Working for a short time as a U.S. deputy marshal, he helped capture the deadly Jim Miller, who had been terrorizing the Southwest.

Once Miller was in custody, Canton's federal commission was canceled. He secured the help of the territorial governor of Oklahoma to find the reason. After much correspondence, a representative of the U.S. Justice Department wrote "that Canton had robbed a bank in Texas and found it necessary to change his name upon coming to Oklahoma. . . . Canton was known as a bad man and had killed a number of people."[44]

If this revelation upset Canton, it was short lived. Timing was on his side as statehood was declared for Oklahoma in 1907. When newly elected governor Charles Haskell had to appoint an adjutant general to form the state's National Guard the following year, he looked no further than Frank Canton. Although he had worked with the military many times, Canton had never spent a day in the military. He proceeded to organize and train his charges, who would eventually be called to deal with civil unrest involving labor disputes, racial tensions, and public riots. Canton did such an im-

Despite having no military training, Frank Canton became an adjutant general in the Oklahoma National Guard in 1907.

pressive job that he was invited to the inauguration of several presidents and remained in his post under three separate governors. In 1917, at age sixty-eight, Canton retired, having served as adjutant general longer than anyone in the history of the state.

Elder Statesman of Law Enforcement

The next ten years of Canton's life were peppered with accolades for his previous service but very little income, since little of his work had garnered a pension. He tried to get his autobiography published, but his health had begun to deteriorate. He celebrated his seventy-eighth birthday quietly at home, and twelve days later, on September 27, 1927, Frank Canton died at his daughter's home. Canton's wife, Annie, was dealt another tragic blow when forty-two-year-old daughter Ruby died the following year of cancer.

Frank Canton's funeral was an elaborate affair that brought out the highest officials in Oklahoma. He was buried with full military honors as befitting a former adjutant general. Charles F. Barrett, then adjutant general, said of Canton in his eulogy, "If I were delegated to write his epitaph, I would put down in the language of that West of which he was a part: 'Here lies a man.'"[45]

Canton's autobiography, titled *Frontier Trails: The Autobiography of Frank Canton*, was finally published in 1930. The author went to great pains to let the reader know it was not ghostwritten, and it proved to be quite a revelation to those who read it: Many of the dignitaries who were present at his funeral discovered for the first time that the man they had honored was none other than Joe Horner.

CHAPTER 5

Pat Garrett: Cursed by the Kid

The life of Pat Garrett was filled with many adventures in a lifetime that encompassed work as a cowboy, buffalo hunter, bartender, sheriff, author, customs agent, and rancher. However, the killing of Billy the Kid, for better or for worse, made him a lawman of legendary status. For Garrett, that one event proved to be more of a detriment than an asset as he tried alternately to live down the episode and cash in on its notoriety.

Patrick Floyd Garrett was born in Chambers County, Alabama, on June 5, 1850, the second of seven children born to farmers John Lumpkin Garrett and Elizabeth Ann Jarvis Garrett. In 1853 John Garrett purchased a Louisiana plantation in Claiborne Parish that made the family quite prominent in the community. Pat grew up in Louisiana, where he received an elementary education but then left school to work the family's farm. His parents both died when they were still fairly young. Pat tried to keep the family farm going, but had a falling-out with a brother-in-law over the estate. Now over six feet tall and slim bodied, the restless eighteen-year-old left Louisiana to see what the western frontier of 1869 had to offer.

The Savagery of the West

Garrett drifted into Fort Griffin, Texas, and found work as a cowboy. He eventually teamed up with a young Kentuckian named Skelton Glenn, and together the two youths roamed the plains hunting buffalo. Unfortunately, the herds were thinning rapidly due to overhunting. Although successful at first, Glenn and Garrett soon found the quickly vanishing buffalo harder and harder to come by.

In November 1876 the now frontier-hardened Garrett had his first major run-in with the savagery of the West. Garrett's skinner (whose job was to skin the dead buffalo), a short, stocky Irishman named Joe Briscoe, grumbled on his way back from the river with his laundry that it was impossible to clean anything in the muddy water. He squatted next to Garrett to warm himself near the campfire, and Garrett off-handedly remarked, "No one but a damned Irishman would be stupid enough to wash anything in that muddy water."[46] Whether it was the bitterly cold morning or the frustration of the hunt, Briscoe angrily swung at Garrett, who avoided the punch and knocked Briscoe down. This went on for some time, with Garrett constantly knocking down the wildly swinging Briscoe. Garrett tried to apologize, which angered his opponent even more. Briscoe grabbed an ax, but before he could swing it, Garrett grabbed his rifle and shot Briscoe dead.

The other hunters knew Garrett was defending himself, but that was little comfort to him. Garrett mounted his horse and rode out to find Glenn, who was hunting on the plains. Taking his partner's advice, Garrett rode to Fort Griffin to turn himself in, but after he explained what happened the authorities declined to prosecute. This episode, followed by an Indian raid, permanently soured Garrett on the idea of buffalo hunting.

He and Glenn rode on and settled in Fort Sumner, New Mexico, in 1877. They went their separate ways, with Garrett staying on and marrying the teenaged Juanita Gutierrez. The union was short lived, as Juanita died a few months later during a miscarriage. Garrett himself was injured when a wild sow trampled him while he was working a hog farm. Juanita's sister Apolinara nursed him back to health, and on January 14, 1880, the two were married. The marriage produced nine children and was by all accounts a happy union.

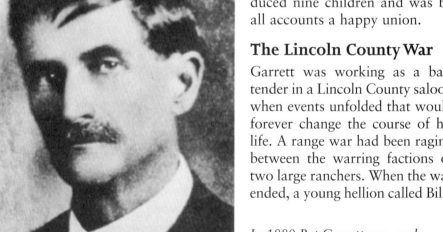

The Lincoln County War

Garrett was working as a bartender in a Lincoln County saloon when events unfolded that would forever change the course of his life. A range war had been raging between the warring factions of two large ranchers. When the war ended, a young hellion called Billy

In 1880 Pat Garrett was made sheriff of Lincoln County, New Mexico, and charged with the task of bringing Billy the Kid to justice.

the Kid was still running afoul of the law. Garrett was not involved in the range war, but he did know Billy the Kid. It is not known exactly when they first met or how well they knew each other; the two may have been passing acquaintances or very good friends.

Garrett was thrust into the limelight because of an endorsement he received from rancher John Chisum. Chisum was one of the big ranchers involved in the range war and had known and liked Garrett for some time. He suggested to territorial governor Lew Wallace that Garrett would be a good man to lead the crusade in rounding up outlaws such as Billy the Kid. Chisum's endorsement set in motion a series of events that led to Garrett being nominated for sheriff.

There is no evidence that Garrett had ever previously considered working as a lawman, but the backing of Wallace and several rich landowners saw Garrett elected sheriff of Lincoln County on November 2, 1880. His success was primarily due to his vow to bring the reign of lawlessness to an end. Wallace had a specific outlaw in mind when he took out an ad in a local newspaper. It read: "I will pay $500 reward to any person or persons who will capture William Bonney, alias Billy the Kid, and deliver him to any sheriff in New Mexico."[47]

Sheriff Pat Garrett

While concerned citizens and newspaper editors complained about what they considered to be a paltry reward for the Kid's capture, Garrett focused on fulfilling his promise of reining in the lawlessness of Lincoln County. His reputation steadily growing, Garrett's mettle was tested publicly after he delivered prisoners to the town of Puerto de Luna. In a local store, a boisterous outlaw named Mariano Leiva accosted Garrett, shouting as he wandered out into the street, "No gringo [white man] can arrest me! By god, even that damned Pat Garrett can't take me!"[48] When Leiva turned back toward the store, Garrett stood in front of him and pushed him into the dirt. Leiva drew his gun and fired wildly, missing his intended target. Garrett drew his gun and shot twice, shattering Leiva's shoulder. He then took Leiva to jail and fined him eighty dollars for attempted murder.

Garrett's main concern as sheriff was capturing Billy the Kid. On December 19, 1880, Garrett and his men almost caught the Kid and his gang, but they eluded capture. The next morning Garrett and his posse surrounded the Kid's gang in a one-room rock house at Stinking Springs, near Fort Sumner. A gunfight erupted when gang member Charlie Bowdre stepped out and was mistaken for the Kid. The wounded Bowdre ran inside but was

After capturing Billy the Kid and his gang in December 1880, Garrett brought them by wagon to Las Vegas, New Mexico.

pushed back out by the Kid. Bowdre was shot again, staggered, and died in Garrett's arms. Garrett and his men decided to wait the Kid out and proceeded to make themselves breakfast. When Garrett asked the Kid how he was holding up, the Kid complained of not having enough wood for breakfast. "Come out and get some. Be a little sociable," replied Garrett.[49]

Hungry and tired, the Kid and his gang surrendered that afternoon. Garrett took the shackled prisoners by buckboard into Las Vegas, New Mexico, where Garrett had to fight off a mob at the train station before he could move them on to the state prison at Santa Fe to await trial. A judge sentenced Billy the Kid on April 15, 1881, to be turned over to Pat Garrett so he could be hanged in Lincoln on May 13.

End of the Line

A little more than a week later, Garrett was out of town delivering some important papers when Billy the Kid escaped from prison, killing two guards in the process. Garrett would later say that the guards had not heeded his warning to take extra precaution in dealing with the prisoner and that the jail in Lincoln was flimsy at best. He did accept partial responsibility for the Kid's escape, saying, "To me, the escape of the Kid was a most distressing calamity for which I do not hold myself guiltless. His escape and the murder of his two guards were the result of mismanagement and carelessness in great measure."[50]

Garrett trailed Billy the Kid for another three months before finally yielding any results. In July 1881, Garrett received a tip that Billy the Kid might show up at the home of their mutual friend Pete Maxwell. On the night of July 13, Garrett and his men arrived shortly after midnight at the Maxwell Ranch. Garrett had two of his men stand guard outside as he went in to talk with Maxwell.

The Kid was indeed on the premises that night for a dance that was held at another part of the ranch. He left to get something to eat at the main house when he saw the men posted outside. Barefoot and hatless, the Kid slipped inside the house through a side entrance. Garrett and Maxwell sat talking in the darkness of the bedroom when Billy the Kid appeared in the doorway with his gun in his hand.

The next several moments forever changed the course of Garrett's life. Neither man immediately recognized the other but sensed each other's presence. As the Kid whispered to Maxwell in Spanish to find out who was in the room, Maxwell identified the Kid to Garrett. The Kid cocked his revolver but Garrett had already stood with his gun drawn and fired a single shot directly into the Kid's heart. Garrett moved aside and fired another shot. He later said, "The second shot was useless; the Kid fell dead. He never spoke. A struggle or two, a little strangling sound as he gasped for breath, and the Kid was with his many victims."[51]

Garrett's Side of the Story

The death of Billy the Kid made national headlines. To his defenders he was a misunderstood youth forced to violence by circumstance. To his detractors he was a dishonorable traitor who cared little for any human life other than his own. Many people grew rich writing about the Kid's exploits, but for Pat Garrett just getting the reward money that was promised him proved to be an ordeal.

Governor W.G. Ritch, who succeeded Wallace, considered his predecessor's reward a personal offer not sanctioned by the office. He publicly stated about Wallace's offer that "there is no record whatever, either in his office or at the Secretary's office, of there having been a reward offered."[52] Garrett hired a lawyer and took legal action to get what he felt he was rightfully owed. In the interim, many citizens—glad to see the end of the Kid—added to the amount. Garrett eventually received more than a thousand dollars. He quickly spent the money on drinking and gambling.

Seeing so many other people making money on the Kid's legend infuriated Garrett. When an old writer friend named Ashton Upson approached him to collaborate on his own version of events, Garrett readily agreed. The result was a book with almost three dozen words in the title, but best remembered simply as *The Authentic Life of Billy the Kid* by Pat Garrett. Published in 1882, the book was not successful and was taken to task for its inaccuracies. The inaccuracies in the text would later be blamed for many of the myths that developed concerning Billy the Kid.

Upson, a self-proclaimed expert on Billy the Kid, wrote the bulk of the book, but the last several chapters were reportedly penned

Billy the Kid killed two guards as he escaped from the Lincoln County courthouse (pictured) in 1881.

On July 13, 1881, Pat Garrett fired a fatal shot directly into Billy the Kid's heart.

by Garrett. The final chapters of the book allowed Garrett to respond to much of the criticism levied against him, such as the widely held opinion that he was afraid to shoot Billy the Kid. He wrote, "Some have claimed that I was scared on this occasion. Scared? Suppose a man of the Kid's noted disposition and temper had warned you that when you and he met you had better 'come a-shooting'? . . . Scared? Well I should say so."[53]

Trying to Move On

The failure of the writing venture and the end of his term as sheriff greatly embittered Garrett. The man who had once been rather affable and friendly to those who knew him began to take every criticism, large or small, as a personal assault. When Garrett tried to run for state senate, a local newspaper ran several letters to the editor denouncing Garrett and accusing him of illiteracy. The author of the letters signed his name as "X." Garrett thought he knew who it was, confronted him, and had a fistfight in the street with the man. What had so upset Garrett was a letter that spoke of him in the following manner: "The newspaper notoriety he received from his success in killing Billy the Kid has upset his brain."[54] It is not known if the man Garrett attacked was indeed X, but the letters stopped showing up in the paper. Garrett lost the election.

In 1890, following a short stint as a Texas Ranger, Garrett ran for sheriff in a reorganized area in New Mexico called Chaves

*After gunning down Billy the Kid (pictured), Garrett published an
account of the showdown that was riddled with inaccuracies.*

County. He may have thought a new county would give him a new start, but that was not the case. He was soundly defeated and even more embittered than he was after the state senate loss. He and his family left New Mexico and tried a new start ranching in Uvalde County, Texas. With the help of a powerful local politician named John Nance Garner, who would go on to become Franklin Roosevelt's first vice president, Garrett was elected a county commissioner in Uvalde and began to regain his self-esteem. For Garrett, the happiest years after the shooting of the Kid were spent on the Uvalde ranch with his wife and children while working for the county commission.

The Mystery of Albert Fountain

The greatest boost Garrett received in reviving his spirits played out in a similar vein as the Billy the Kid scenario. An important New Mexico businessman named Albert Fountain and his nine-year-old son, Henry, disappeared one cold January night in 1896. An investigation discovered their wagon tracks, as well as those of three other horses and dried blood. A fury of controversy quickly developed over the presumed murders, and territorial governor William Thornton was forced to act. He offered a two-thousand-dollar reward and had Garrett appointed sheriff of Dona Ana County, with the sole purpose of catching the culprits.

Garrett set his sights on Oliver Lee, an ally of Fountain's political rival, and a henchman named Jim Gililland. Over the next several years, Garrett was frustrated in gathering enough evidence, but he did eventually bring the two into custody to face prosecution. The pair's lawyer was A.B. Fall, the political rival of Fountain. His lengthy defense concluded with the words, "You would not hang a yellow dog on the evidence presented here, much less two men."[55] The courtroom burst into applause and fifteen minutes later the men were acquitted. Garrett finished out his term as sheriff and then moved to a ranch in the San Andres Mountains.

U.S. Customs Officer

In December 1901 President Theodore Roosevelt appointed Pat Garrett U.S. customs collector in El Paso, Texas. Garrett was a controversial appointment, but Roosevelt was a great fan of western heroes and considered the killer of Billy the Kid a living legend. Garrett almost immediately came under fire for rudeness and unprofessional behavior. At one point he got into a public brawl with a man he had fired and then thought had slandered his name. Secretary of the Treasury Leslie Shaw requested that Garrett give a report to defend his actions. In response Garrett wrote, "Although my side of the case has not been presented, and you say that I was entirely in the wrong and have no defense, I do not see where any report by me would be considered by you as justifiable for my conduct."[56]

The matter was then dropped, but Garrett found himself in trouble again when he managed to get an unsavory character named Tom Powers to pose in a picture with the president without Roosevelt's knowledge. When Garrett was to be reappointed in 1905, Roosevelt refused to do so, forcing Garrett and his family to return to New Mexico.

The Strange Death of Pat Garrett

Depression and tragedy mark the final years of Pat Garrett. He returned to New Mexico and bought a horse ranch, but it turned out to be a bad investment. Under great financial strain, he was

Pat Garrett was murdered shortly after this photo was taken in 1908. The identity of the murderer has never been proven.

forced to lease the land out to a man named Wayne Brazel, but regretted the decision when Brazel brought goats to graze the land. Garrett felt this was in breach of their agreement and a bitter feud developed. Garrett wanted to lease the land to a man of questionable character named Carl Adamson. James P. Miller, a cousin of Adamson, offered to purchase the Garrett ranch. However, Miller said he did not want the goats, and Wayne Brazel refused to either move them or cancel the five-year lease.

These complexities may have been a ruse to swindle Garrett out of his land. The ongoing conflict and lack of funds greatly depressed the fifty-eight-year-old Garrett. In a letter to a friend he wrote, "Pardon the unintelligent manner in which this letter is written for I am suffering great distress of mind and soul."[57]

The conflict reached a tragic conclusion on February 29, 1908. Garrett had requested a meeting in Las Cruces with all the concerned parties to reach a satisfactory conclusion. Adamson and Garrett rode in a buckboard while Brazel was on horseback alongside the wagon. An argument ensued during the trip when Miller appeared to join the trio. Garrett stopped the buckboard to get out and urinate. When he turned, two gunshots blasted him in the back of the head.

Brazel confessed to the killing, claiming self-defense, but he was acquitted due to lack of evidence. Many felt he confessed to cover for Miller, who was lynched the same day Brazel was acquitted. Adamson was jailed for smuggling immigrants, leaving many questions left unanswered. It may never be known who actually killed Pat Garrett, the man who shot Billy the Kid.

CHAPTER 6

Bat Masterson: Killer Reputation

The life of lawman Bat Masterson was often as wild as the times in which he lived. Unlike his friend Wyatt Earp, Masterson was not mythologized through a single famous incident; rather, almost every new turn in his life seemed to contribute to his legendary status. Masterson exploited his experiences to create a reputation that often seems too amazing to be true. This reputation may have served Masterson well in dealing with the unsavory elements of the West, but it also resulted in many embellishments that Masterson did little to set straight.

Yearning for Adventure

William Bartholomew Masterson was born in Henryville, Quebec, Canada, on November 26, 1853. He was the second of seven children born to Thomas and Catherine Masterson. He later legally changed his middle name to Barclay, but from early childhood everyone called him Bat. The Mastersons moved to the United States and eventually settled on a farm near Wichita, Kansas. His younger brother Tom remembered Bat as yearning for adventure at an early age. "Bat could never sit in a classroom if he could slip out while the teacher wasn't looking, grab his rifle, whistle for his dog and come home with meat for the table,"[58] he said.

In the fall and winter of 1871, eighteen-year-old Bat and his older brother, Ed, headed west to hunt buffalo. They camped with other hunters and met several future western legends, including Wyatt Earp, who would become Masterson's lifelong friend. In the summer of the following year, the Masterson brothers worked for the railroad in the area that would become Dodge City. When the job was finished their boss vanished, creating the first of many Masterson legends. Masterson later caught up with the man and collected their wages either by fisticuffs or at gunpoint. That winter the Mastersons again hunted buffalo and were joined by their younger brother Jim. They shot and butchered up to twenty buffalo a day until the herds moved on and the Masterson brothers temporarily went their separate ways.

From Adobe Walls to Living Legend

Masterson, on his own at this point, was in the Texas panhandle town of Adobe Walls on June 26, 1874. The town was so named because it comprised several adobe buildings slapped together haphazardly to accommodate the transient buffalo hunters. Shortly after Masterson's arrival three different Native American tribes, led by Comanche chief Quanna Parker, attacked the area. The Native Americans were angered over the many buffalo that had been slaughtered. Their attack on Adobe Walls was met by a mere handful of hunters.

William "Bat" Masterson hunted buffalo and worked on the railroad before becoming a lawman in Dodge City.

It proved to be enough. Masterson and three dozen other hunters kept them at bay for a full week until U.S. Army troops arrived. Over time, the number of Native Americans reported to have been involved in the attack grew from several hundred to several thousand, adding to Masterson's growing reputation. Whatever the actual number was, the army officer in charge, Colonel Nelson Miles, was so impressed with Masterson he offered him a job as scout, which was quickly accepted. By March 1875 Masterson was in Dodge City, where he was listed in the Kansas census as a teamster.

Early the next year he was involved in an altercation in the town of Sweetwater, Texas. There are several versions of what took place on the night of January 24. What is known is that in the Lady Gay Dance Hall, Masterson was in the company of a young woman named Mollie Brennan. An angry soldier named Melvin King entered the dance hall, and several gunshots were fired. When the smoke cleared King lay dead, Brennan bled to death, and Masterson had a bullet lodged in his pelvis. He was nursed back to health, but a painful limp required the use of a cane that would become part of his legend. It is likely that King was the only man Bat Masterson ever killed. What actually transpired remains a mystery, but Masterson emerged with an even greater reputation as a man not to be trifled with.

Becoming a Dodge City Lawman

The next summer, twenty-three-year-old Masterson returned to Dodge City. Aside from his skill with a gun, he was quickly gaining a reputation as a gambler and invested in a saloon that allowed him to indulge his passion to his heart's content. Brothers Jim and Ed were also living in Dodge as a saloon owner and assistant marshal, respectively. Bat Masterson's presence in the rowdy cow town drew more attention than that of his brothers. With his brightly colored sash, neckerchief, and silver-plated holster, he drew stares wherever he went.

Shortly after his arrival, Masterson ran afoul of the law, in this case a three-hundred-pound city marshal named Larry Deger. Deger was escorting a man named Bobby Gill to jail on charges of public drunkenness. Deger kicked Gill several times along the way, and what happened next, according to the *Dodge City Times*, caught Deger off guard: "This act was soon interrupted by Bat Masterson who wound his arm affectionately around the marshal's neck and let the prisoner escape."[59] The two men grappled as several Texas cowboys came to Deger's aid. Masterson was beaten severely and taken to jail, while Ed Masterson brought Gill in the next day. Gill was escorted out of town but, as the brother of a city official, Masterson paid only a heavy fine.

Mayor James Kelley of Dodge City took a liking to Masterson. He got the city council to lower the fine and made Masterson a tempting offer. Holding a bitter grudge over the beating he took from Larry Deger, Masterson agreed to Kelley's proposition to become a deputy under Ford County sheriff Charlie Bassett. Kelley then helped mount Masterson's campaign to replace the retiring Bassett. In November 1877 Masterson was elected Ford County Sheriff, defeating his opponent, Larry Deger, by just three votes.

Sheriff Bat Masterson

Masterson's tenure as sheriff was highlighted by incidents as colorful as the man himself. Two months after his election, he impressed the citizens of Dodge City by capturing a band of train robbers without firing a single shot. He did it using dogged determination and a keen instinct. He trailed the robbers without their knowledge and, one by one, brought them all into custody. One of them was "Dirty" Dave Rudabaugh, who would later escape from prison and gain infamy in Billy the Kid's gang.

As sheriff of Dodge, Masterson also underwent a major metamorphosis. Gone was the gaudy clothing of his youth, replaced by the fashionable attire of the day, which added to his reputation as a dignified dandy. Although he no longer needed it, Masterson strolled the streets of Dodge twirling his cane, adorned in a tailor-made three-piece black suit and a small bowler hat with a curled brim. Comedian Eddie Foy, who often played Dodge City, described the sheriff's appearance: "A trim, good-looking young man with a pleasant face and carefully barbered mustache, well-tailored clothes, hat with a rakish tilt, and two big silver-mounted, ivory-handled pistols in a heavy belt."[60]

Masterson used more than just his fashionable appearance to execute the responsibilities of his office. His personal style was a preference toward talking his adversaries out of trouble rather than fighting with them, often practicing his gun prowess publicly to make his point. It helped that he had the support of such respected deputies as retired sheriff Charlie Bassett, Wyatt Earp, Luke Short, and Bill Tilghman, as well as the friendship of such gunmen as Ben Thompson and Doc Holliday. Anyone who sought to tangle with Masterson ran the risk of a follow-up visit by any of these legendary men.

As sheriff of Dodge City, Masterson (right) had the help of many famous deputies, including Wyatt Earp (left).

After a while, Masterson and his deputies found it took very little to subdue a troublemaking cowboy. This was because previous cowboys, ambushed and brought into jail to sleep off a drunken night before being sent home, and too embarrassed to admit they had been ambushed, embellished the reputation of the Dodge City lawmen in an effort to save face. According to noted western historian Robert DeArment, "When such miscreants returned to their home ranges, they spread lurid tales of the lawmen who had clapped a tight lid on Dodge. They exaggerated out of all proportions the gunslinging records of Masterson, Earp & Company in an effort to minimize the ignominy of their own arrests."[61]

The Murders of Ed Masterson and Dora Hand

Not all those who wreaked havoc in Dodge gave in so quietly. In April 1878 Bat's brother Ed, now a full marshal, made a terrible mistake that cost him his life. He confronted a drunken cowboy named Walker and asked for the gun he was shooting all over town. Ed Masterson then gave the firearm to the cowboy's nearby friend, who returned it to its owner. Walker fired at Ed Masterson at such close range that the flare from the muzzle ignited the marshal's coat on fire. Masterson was able to shoot and kill his assailant, but his own wounds were fatal. Bat Masterson ran to his brother's side, but the elder Masterson succumbed thirty minutes later.

There was an investigation into the shooting to discover exactly what had transpired. Masterson, devastated by his brother's murder, gave testimony that was later interpreted to mean that he had shot his brother's assailant. Many years later, writers would add colorful details of how he had gunned down the man who killed his brother.

Masterson did little to prevent these stories from adding to his reputation, choosing instead to elaborate on his gun-handling technique. He let it be known humorously how he and others modified their weapons: "We used to file the notch of the hammer till the trigger would pull sweet, which is another way of saying that the blamed gun would pretty near go off if you looked at it."[62]

In October 1878 Masterson led one of the most famous posses ever assembled. A young man named James Kennedy, twice arrested for drunkenness by Earp and Bassett, was severely beaten by Kelley the next time he arrived in Dodge to see his lover, Dora Hand. Kennedy rode into Dodge late the next morning and fired several shots into Kelley's window. Kelley had left town on early business, but Kennedy's wild shooting spree killed Dora Hand, sleeping in the hotel next door. Masterson organized a posse, consisting of Bill Tilghman, Wyatt Earp, Charlie Bassett, and several others, to catch the fleeing Kennedy. When the posse reached the fugitive a short gunfight ensued, killing Kennedy's horse and shattering his shoulder. When Masterson told him of the death of Dora Hand, Kennedy quietly sobbed, "I wish you had killed me."[63]

A Bitter Exit

Although he did not know it at the time, 1879 would be Masterson's final year as sheriff. It started as a tumultuous year with the successful capture of a horse thief he pursued all the way to Colorado. In February Masterson brought seven Cheyenne held in Leavenworth to stand trial in Dodge for a raid they had committed the previous fall. The transfer of the prisoners by train and wagon was expensive and fraught with meddlesome crowds. The trial ended with the charges being dropped for lack of evidence.

In this 1890 photo, Bat Masterson (rear, far right) is pictured with his deputies, including Charlie Bassett, Wyatt Earp, and Luke Short (front, left to right).

Things settled down considerably during the remainder of the year, but when reelection time came around in November, Masterson's term was in jeopardy. In spite of his many accomplishments, especially in dealing with horse thieves, public opinion had turned against him. His expenses for bringing in the Cheyenne prisoners, more than four thousand dollars, were charged to the city for reimbursement. This did not sit well with many voters in Dodge, who elected George T. Hinkle, an associate of Larry Deger, as the new sheriff.

Masterson was bitterly disappointed by the defeat. Although he moved on to points west after the election, he never forgot the outcome of that race. Thirty years later, a man introduced himself to Masterson as the son of George Hinkle. The much older Masterson replied, "No doubt you are the son of George Hinkle. Which one of his women was your mother?"[64]

Battle of the Plaza

Bat Masterson's life after his tenure as sheriff of Ford County was rather tame by comparison. He traveled throughout several western states, gambling and answering the call to help any number of friends who requested his assistance. He helped gunfighter Ben Thompson's brother Billy out of Nebraska when he was wounded in a gunfight and in danger of being lynched. He went to Tombstone, Arizona, to visit with Wyatt Earp in 1881 but was called away by his brother Jim. The call kept Masterson out of the gunfight at the O.K. Corral.

Jim Masterson's urgent telegraph to his brother was of the utmost importance. Jim had also served as a Dodge City lawman for a short time, but in 1881 his part-ownership of a local saloon was developing into a bitter feud. His partner, A.J. Peacock, angrily disagreed with Jim over an employee (and Peacock's brother-in-law) named Al Updegraff, whom Jim accused of drinking on the job. The conflict grew to threatening proportions, forcing Jim to call his brother for assistance.

On the train ride back to Dodge, Bat feared that the fate of his brother Ed would be repeated with Jim before he could get there. Fearing an ambush, Masterson got off the train before it pulled into the station and walked toward the back of the slowing caboose. In the street on the other side of town were Peacock and Updegraff, and in short order gunfire broke out. Masterson dug in behind the high grade of the track embankment and fired back, while his assailants took cover beside the nearby jail located on the other side of the tracks. The patrons of a nearby

Bat Masterson took part in a shootout in this Dodge City plaza when he intervened in a fight between his brother and a former business partner.

saloon also began shooting at Updegraff and Peacock. Updegraff soon fell forward with a bullet wound to the chest, and Peacock surrendered when he ran out of bullets. Once he learned that his brother was unharmed, Masterson surrendered himself to Mayor Ab Webster. Legend would later say that Masterson killed his assailants, but both men survived what came to be called the Battle of the Plaza.

An Exaggerated Reputation

The popularity of the Mastersons was at an all-time low as Bat and Jim were told in no uncertain terms to get out of Dodge. The shootout with Updegraff and Peacock may have angered the citizens of Dodge, but it went a long way toward exaggerating Bat Masterson's already inflated reputation. It remains doubtful that Masterson actually shot Updegraff, who was out of striking distance. The logical culprit was an unidentified saloon patron.

None of this mattered when Masterson was seen in Dodge again two years later. His very presence in town helped end what became known as the Saloon Wars. Masterson's friend Luke Short was in conflict with other saloon owners in Dodge and was also told to leave town. Staying in Kansas City, Short sent telegraphs to his old friends requesting their help and waited as word of their arrival gained momentum. The local newspaper wrote: "At the head is Bat Masterson. He is credited with having killed one man for every year of his life. This may be exaggerated, but he is certainly entitled to a record of a dozen or more. He is a cool, brave man, pleasant in his manners, but terrible in a fight."[65] The peaceful presence in town of Masterson, Earp, Holliday, and several others was all that was needed to bring about an amicable solution to the conflict.

Masterson continued to roam, serving briefly as a lawman in Colorado but earning most of his money gambling throughout the West. On November 21, 1891, five days before his thirty-seventh birthday, he married former saloon girl Emma Walters, who tolerated his behavior for the next thirty years. Emma was often present when strangers requested one of her husband's guns with notches of victories filed into the metal. Masterson would simply purchase a used Colt .45 in a gun shop and carve twenty-two notches in it. The first time he did this the shocked collector asked Masterson if he had really killed that many men. Masterson later said, "I didn't tell him yes, and I didn't tell him no, and I didn't exactly lie to him . . . and he went away tickled to death."[66]

Quitting the West

At the turn of the century, Masterson had apparently had his fill of the West and decided to settle in New York City. His gambling interest had developed into a love of sports that sent him east to promote several professional boxing matches. He quickly made friends with some of the most influential people in America, including President Theodore Roosevelt. A writer named Alfred Henry Lewis convinced the former lawman to write about his Old West experiences. Masterson agreed to write sketches about the other legends he knew only if Lewis wrote the chapter about Masterson. Masterson's writing helped to expand the popular image of the western lawman by describing the attributes he felt were required to be successful. He wrote that the three most important factors to staying alive were courage, proficient knowledge of guns, and, most important, deliberation: "I have known men in the West whose courage could not be questioned and whose expertness with the pistol was simply marvelous, who fell easy victims before men who added deliberation to the other two qualities."[67] Such statements went a long way in contributing to his own reputation.

The writing venture proved so successful that Masterson acquired a job on the *New York Telegraph* as a sportswriter and columnist, eventually becoming president of the newspaper. He wrote his daily column in the morning, mingled with New York's elite and infamous in the afternoon, and dined in fashionable restaurants with Emma every night. In 1905 Roosevelt also appointed him U.S. marshal in New York, but the position was revoked during the Taft administration.

Masterson spent his remaining days as a popular but curmudgeonly New York character who occasionally drank too much and sometimes held opinions that ran afoul of others. When another reporter challenged Masterson's opinion in a populated eatery, the legend of the West put his hand in his coat pocket, scattering the reporter and others, who expected gunfire. When a friend later asked Masterson if he would have really shot the man, Masterson reached into the same pocket and pulled out a pack of cigarettes.

On October 25, 1921, sixty-seven-year-old Bat Masterson was found dead at his desk, the victim of a heart attack. In the typewriter was his last column, which was printed the day of his funeral. It read, in part: "There are those who argue that everything breaks even in this old dump of a world of ours. I suppose the ginks [guys] who argue that way hold that, because the rich man gets ice in the summer and the poor man gets it in the winter, things are breaking even for both. Maybe so, but I'll swear I can't see it that way."[68]

CHAPTER 7

Bill Tilghman: Last of the Frontier Lawmen

Bat Masterson and Wyatt Earp are the names most people think of when considering legendary lawmen of the West. However, in their day, the lawman whose name was most revered was Bill Tilghman. A contemporary of both Masterson and Earp, Tilghman's career lasted much longer and as such encountered staggering changes. He contributed to the transformation of the western lawman from one who just kept the peace to one who required the knowledge and practice of criminal procedure. Along the way he confronted some of the most dangerous elements any lawman could face. In writing about the lawman of the West, Bat Masterson said, "Tilghman was the greatest of us all."[69]

Frontier Experiences

William Matthew Tilghman Jr. was born July 4, 1854, in Fort Dodge, Iowa. His Independence Day birthdate was fortuitous in a family that included a member of the first Continental Congress; coincidentally, it was also his father's birthday. William Tilghman Sr. and his wife, Amanda, raised two other sons and three daughters on the money they made selling goods to the U.S. Army at Ford Dodge. When the fort was closed down, the Tilghmans moved to Minnesota, finally settling on a farm in Atcheson, Kansas. Along the way, Bill had his first encounter with the dangers of the frontier. While he was nestled in his mother's arms during a Native American attack, an arrow cut through Amanda Tilghman's sleeve and lodged in the buckboard just inches from the baby's head.

When the Civil War broke out, Bill's father became the head of a Union company and eight-year-old Bill took on the responsibility of head of the household. He farmed with his mother and attended a one-room schoolhouse. After the war ended, Bill stayed on until the spring of 1871, when, at the age of sixteen, he traversed the Kansas plains to hunt buffalo.

Tilghman's experiences hunting buffalo helped harden the young man to life on the frontier. He quickly developed a reputation as an accurate and deadly marksman. On a cold New Year's Day in 1874, Tilghman was asked to demonstrate his prowess with the heavy Sharps buffalo rifle. He impressed even veteran plainsmen by downing a buffalo nearly a mile away with a single shot. Cheyenne chief Roman Nose, also at the demonstration, was equally impressed with Tilghman's marksmanship.

Some sources claim that at this time the young Tilghman fell in with a bad crowd, with names like Hurricane Bill and Dutch Henry, who took advantage of Roman Nose's hospitality. Tilghman and his cohorts allegedly stole horses and cattle from the Native American reservation but were not charged due to lack of evidence. He had several other close calls with both the law and Native Americans in his early days on the frontier. Tilghman then made a conscious effort to change his ways by working as an army scout until 1877.

He had another run-in with the law the following year, when he was arrested as a suspect in a train robbery. Ten days later, Tilghman was released and the charges were dropped. The prosecuting attorney went so far as to write Tilghman an open letter of apology, which was printed in the *Dodge City Times*. It said, in part, "I congratulate you on your discharge, hoping that you may be so lucky in the future as not to be ever suspected of crime."[70] Tilghman heeded the advice by working hard to build a reputation of honest respectability that would remain for the rest of his life.

A New Kind of Lawman

One of the major headquarters for the buffalo hunters at that time was Dodge City, and it was there that Tilghman began his career as a lawman. He met and married Flora Kendall in 1878, and together they started a farm outside Dodge City not far from the Arkansas River. Dodge City's new sheriff was Bat Masterson, Tilghman's friend from his buffalo hunting days. When Masterson offered him a job as deputy, Tilghman readily accepted. After he lost his farm to fire, Tilghman turned to law enforcement full time.

Tilghman learned much by observing his old friend Masterson, but he wanted to do more than just keep drunken cowboys from celebrating too much after a cattle drive. He approached city attorney Mike Sutton about learning the law and its complicated procedures. Sutton agreed and took the young lawman on as a fledgling student. Tilghman did what Masterson and the officials required of him, but on his own, he absorbed the intricacies of frontier law as it applied to his new profession.

Bill Tilghman (left) holds his Sharps rifle, the weapon he used as a crack-shot buffalo hunter in Kansas.

When a horse thief left Dodge for Texas to avoid prosecution, Tilghman undertook the process to have the man legally extradited back to Kansas. It took some time, but Tilghman trailed the shocked horse thief to Texas and then knocked the combatant prisoner unconscious for the ride back to Dodge. Tilghman gave the extradition papers to the equally shocked Texas marshal. "All this trouble for a horse thief? Why didn't you just shoot him?"[71] the marshal asked.

Tilghman earned the respect of his superiors and was well liked in town. He had learned the difference between following the letter of the law and doing what best suited the situation. One of the

Dave Mather (pictured) was a notorious frontier gunman, but Bill Tilghman persuaded him to leave Dodge City without firing a shot.

most notorious men of the Old West, "Mysterious" Dave Mather, ran afoul of the law in Dodge after firing his gun in a revival meeting, sending the participants running for cover. Tilghman managed to take Mather aside and talk him into leaving town. Much to everyone's surprise there were no repercussions, as Mather never returned to Dodge again.

Kansas to Oklahoma

In 1884 Tilghman was made Dodge City marshal, a position he held for the next two years. His badge as city marshal was different than that of any other marshal before him or since. The citizens of Dodge made the badge out of two twenty-dollar gold pieces and had it specially engraved. The inscription read: "William Tilghman, from your many friends. Dodge City, 1884."[72]

The outpouring of respect shown to Tilghman was earned. Other notable lawmen had worked hard to maintain the peace in Dodge City, but they had left by the time Tilghman was made marshal. It was Bill Tilghman who established and successfully maintained the law prohibiting the carrying of firearms of any kind within city limits. Like his predecessors, Tilghman also left Dodge when the cattle drives moved to other Kansas towns. Tilghman's time in Dodge as a lawman came at the end of the town's wilder days, but the changes he instituted remained in effect long after he was gone.

In 1889 Tilghman joined those on the frontier when word spread of the availability of government land. Leaving his wife and two children in Dodge, Tilghman entered the next phase of frontier expansion by moving to Oklahoma to partake of the Oklahoma Land Rush. He staked a claim during the first rush in the town of Perry, and then later in what is now Guthrie. He was also made Perry's first chief of police and dealt with the challenge of organizing a new community.

The Three Guardsmen

The West was entering a new and final stage of expansion. Previous growth had been the result of the transitional cattle industry or the even greater transition that came with the discovery of gold and other precious metals. When these booms dried up, people moved on. The prospect of a land rush was radically different, bringing with it settlers who sought permanent roots in a less transitional community. The land in Oklahoma had been given to the Native Americans, but it was also the stomping ground of many wanted outlaws. As the western frontier seemed to be closing, the acts of the outlaws became even more desperate. Settlers were forced to either aid the likes of the Dalton and Doolin gangs or face tragic consequences.

By 1892 it had become so dangerous that President Grover Cleveland was besieged with requests from settlers to take immediate action. He appointed Everett Nix U.S. marshal and charged him with cleaning up the territory. Nix decided to make three men his deputies. In a short time they were known throughout the West as the Three Guardsmen.

The three men had extremely diverse backgrounds. Chris Madsen was a European immigrant who participated in the history of three different nations. Born and raised in Denmark, he fought with Garibaldi in Italy and later served in the French Foreign Legion. He came to the United States in 1870 and fought in the cavalry during the Indian Wars. Henry Thomas earned the nickname Heck, since that was the most obscene word anyone ever heard the veteran lawman utter. His lack of foul language aside, Georgia-born Thomas was well known in the territory as a private detective. He and Madsen were both marshals for Judge Isaac Parker's federal court when Nix approached them with the appointment. Rounding out the trinity was Bill Tilghman, so well known that Oklahomans had taken to calling him "Uncle Billy."

At the time of his U.S. deputy appointment, Bill Tilghman was in the process of moving his family from Kansas to his new property in Oklahoma. Nix had told his three deputies they would be responsible as a team for cleaning up an area called Hell's Half Acre. It was in fact an area near Perry that had 110 saloons serving a population of 25,000. This averaged out to about one saloon for every 225 people, causing problems on a regular basis. It took the Three Guardsmen close to twenty years to bring civility to the community.

King of the Oklahoma Outlaws

Part of the reason it took so long was a more pressing responsibility Nix had given them. Nix split them up in pursuit of Bill Doolin, dubbed "King of the Oklahoma Outlaws" by Tilghman, and his gang. Doolin and his men had been part of the Dalton Gang but branched out on their own when the Dalton brothers were shot by lawmen in Coffeyville, Kansas. Doolin was responsible for the theft of more than $175,000 in bank and train robberies and his men had well-earned nicknames like Dynamite Dick and Bitter Creek Newcomb.

In 1894 Tilghman and Nix, aided by informants, discovered the Doolin Gang was in Ingalls, Oklahoma, and planned a strategy.

Tilghman was not involved in the event at Ingalls, but it was a bloody affair that left men wounded or dead on both sides. The trail of Doolin had gone cold, leaving the Three Guardsmen to start from scratch.

Tilghman spent the next year and a half doggedly pursuing Doolin, coming close several times. In late 1894 he managed to wound gang member Bill Raidler as the gang made their escape. Raidler was in too much pain to travel, so Tilghman nursed him back to health until he could ride. He later helped Raidler get paroled. At one point, Tilghman and his deputies missed Doolin by less than twenty minutes after the outlaws had breakfast at a local farm. Knowing the law was close on his tail, Doolin informed the farmer that Tilghman would pay for breakfast, which Tilghman begrudgingly did once he reached the farm.

On more than one occasion, the hunt for Doolin almost cost Tilghman his life. Following up on a tip, Tilghman approached a ranch house on a cold January night in 1895. While his deputy waited outside, Tilghman en-

Henry Thomas, known as "Heck" served with Bill Tilghman for thirty-five years as a deputy marshal in Indian Territory.

tered the ranch house and saw a man warming himself by the fire. When the man refused to answer any questions, Tilghman casually glanced at the tiers of bunks that surrounded him. As Tilghman slowly walked out, he noted that each bunk contained a gun muzzle aimed directly at him. He learned later that it was indeed the Doolin Gang and, as gang member Red Buck watched Tilghman get in his wagon, Doolin reportedly lowered Buck's rifle and said, "Bill Tilghman is too good a man to be shot in the back."[73]

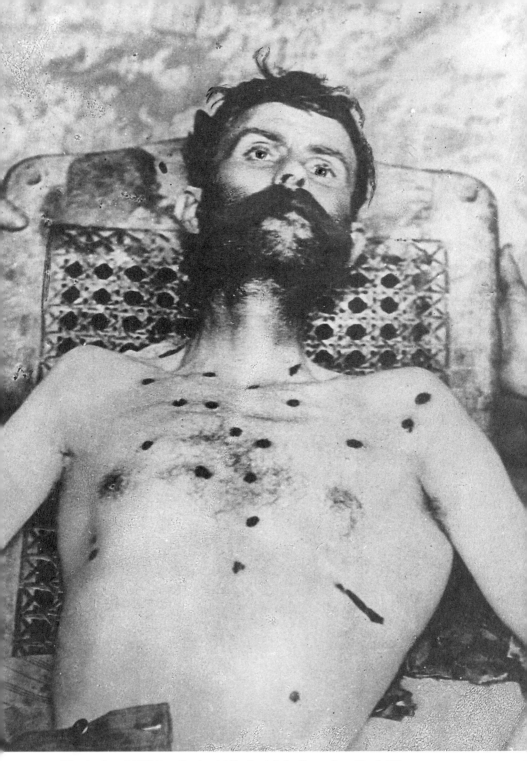

The body of Bill Doolin is riddled with bullets after Heck Thomas gunned down the outlaw in 1896.

It was not long after this close call that Tilghman again encountered Doolin. Based again on an informer's tip, Tilghman traveled to Eureka Springs, Arkansas, where Doolin had gone to treat his rheumatism. As Doolin sat soaking in the therapeutic hot baths, Tilghman approached him with gun in hand. The outlaw surrendered after a short scuffle and Tilghman immediately brought him back to Oklahoma. At the Arkansas train station Tilghman wired Nix: "I have him. Will be home tomorrow."[74]

Sheriff of Lincoln County, Oklahoma

The success of bringing in Bill Doolin was short lived. The outlaw escaped in August of the same year. Tilghman had high hopes of collecting the five-thousand-dollar reward on Doolin, one of the largest ever offered at the time. Unfortunately, the reward stipulated Doolin had to be both captured and convicted, making it impossible for Tilghman to collect. Doolin was later shot and killed by Heck Thomas near Lawson, Oklahoma.

Capturing Doolin made Tilghman famous, but he did not rest on his laurels. Vigilantism had long been a problem on the frontier, and Bill Tilghman may be the first lawman to actively confront it. In 1898 two innocent Native American boys were lynched and burned by a mob that believed the boys had raped and murdered a white woman. The story made national headlines as Tilghman not only pursued and arrested members of the mob, but managed to get convictions and long prison terms for eight of them. This proved to be the first time a lynch mob was ever brought to justice in the West. Tilghman then went a step further: He sought out the real rapist-murderer based on physical evidence and captured him as well. Tilghman's efforts went a long way in stemming the tide of mob violence in the Old West.

Tilghman had garnered national praise for his dealing with the lynch mob and used it in pursuit of public office. In 1900 he ran for sheriff in Lincoln County, Oklahoma, and easily won. His work as sheriff was just as impressive as his previous accomplishments. When he ran for reelection, he was able to boast an impressive record in the ads he took out in the local newspaper. Such techniques in campaigning for sheriff were relatively new, but have since become a staple of election campaigns. Tilghman's ad said in part, "During his term of office 84 persons were convicted and sentenced . . . being more than has ever been sent to the penitentiary before or since his term as sheriff."[75]

Frontier Politics

Bill Tilghman's personal life went through some major changes around the turn of the century. His wife, Flora, had been sick for some time and passed away in 1899 of tuberculosis. Three years later, forty-eight-year-old Tilghman married nineteen-year-old school-teacher Zoe Stratton, with whom he spent the remainder of his life.

President Theodore Roosevelt sought Tilghman out for a special mission in 1905. He was to catch a fugitive who had embezzled a large sum of money from a railroad company and was hiding out in Mexico. Tilghman trailed the fugitive on his own, without the help of Mexican authorities. A few weeks later, he surprised the embezzler in a restaurant by pointing a gun to his head. When his prisoner moved his hand toward a gun concealed in his pocket, Tilghman whispered, "Don't try it. I'm pretty good with this thing."[76] Tilghman's capture secured the fugitive's conviction.

Oklahoma was granted statehood in 1907 partly because of Tilghman's efforts to clean up the territory. With such an amazing record, it was not long before Tilghman was asked to run for higher office. He retired as sheriff of Lincoln County and resigned his almost twenty-year commission as a U.S. deputy marshal to run for the Oklahoma state legislature in 1910. Tilghman served one term in the senate when a more desirable offer came along: He was made chief of police in the new state's capital, Oklahoma City, holding the position for almost ten years.

As chief of police he witnessed firsthand the many changes of the new century. Automobiles clogged the streets, electric lights and tele-phone lines appeared throughout the state, and new businesses took hold that had never existed before. Through a business associate Tilghman became involved in the new medium of motion pictures, di-recting and costarring in a silent film called *Passing of the Oklahoma Outlaws* in 1915. The film also starred Chris Madsen and former Oklahoma outlaw and gubernatorial candidate Al Jennings. To en-sure the film's success, Tilghman printed up handbills announcing that he would lecture about his career after each showing. The an-nouncement read in part, "It is a wonderful and thrilling picture and well worth the time of any one to witness."[77] Wherever Tilghman spoke, huge crowds appeared.

Answering the Call

Proud of his record, Tilghman retired from public service in 1922. His retirement years were to be spent at his home in Guthrie in the com-pany of his family, but Oklahoma called him back. Two years after he retired, the town of Cromwell was experiencing unrelenting criminal activity. This small oil boomtown was overrun with Prohibition-era bootleggers and drug smugglers. The town leaders put in a call to Tilghman, hoping he would become their chief of police. Now seventy-one years old and in failing health, Tilghman seriously considered the position. Friends and family advised him not to do it, but Tilghman seemed poised to strap on his guns again. Madsen advised him not to do it, to which Tilghman replied, "Better to die in a gunfight than in bed someday like a woman. . . . I should have things straightened out in a month or so."[78]

Shortly after he arrived in Cromwell, Tilghman sought out the town's criminal ringleader and soon concentrated

Bill Tilghman was shot dead in 1924 at the age of seventy-one while trying to arrest an allegedly corrupt federal officer.

on a presumed crooked federal officer named Wiley Lynn. Lynn was supposed to end the illegal sale of liquor and narcotics in town, but Tilghman believed he was allowing it to flourish. After a few months on the job, a drunken Lynn confronted Tilghman on a public street. Tilghman seized a loaded gun from Lynn, but did not know he carried another weapon. Lynn shot Tilghman in the stomach. Tilghman staggered, walked to a nearby store, and died several minutes later. Lynn was tried for Tilghman's murder but was found not guilty, on grounds of self-defense.

In the years since Tilghman's death, his name has been largely overlooked in the annals of popular culture that celebrate the time in which he lived. In Oklahoma he remains a beloved hero. Every October the state holds a one-day Bill Tilghman festival described as "a celebration of the life and service of legendary lawman Bill Tilghman. This events honors all lawmen."[79] The festival, which takes place in the town of Cromwell, is sponsored by the Bill Tilghman Foundation.

Notes

Introduction: Neither Saints nor Sinners

1. Quoted in "The Wild Wild West," June 1997. www.gunslinger.com/west.html.

Chapter 1: Why the West Was Wild

2. Quoted in Floyd B. Streeter, *Prairie Trails & Cow Towns: The Opening of the Old West*. New York: Devin Adair, 1963, p. 155.

3. Robert R. Dykstra, *The Cattle Towns*. New York: Knopf, 1968, p. 6.

4. Quoted in James D. Horan, *The Authentic Wild West, The Lawmen*. New York: Crown, 1980, p. 5.

5. Lee A. Silva, *Wyatt Earp: A Biography of the Legend*, vol. 1, *The Cowtown Years*. Santa Ana, CA: Graphic Publishers, 2002, p. 246.

6. Bat Masterson, *Famous Gunfighters of the Western Frontier*. Olympic Valley, CA: Outbooks, 1978, p. 4.

Chapter 2: Isaac Parker: The Hanging Judge

7. Quoted in Roger H. Tuller, *Let No Guilty Man Escape: A Judicial Biography of "Hanging Judge" Isaac C. Parker*. Norman: University of Oklahoma Press, 2001, pp. 14–15.

8. Quoted in Eric Leonard, "Biography of Judge Parker," August 2002, Fort Smith National Historic Site. www.nps.gov/fosm/history/judgeparker/bio/bio3.htm.

9. Quoted in Paul Trachtman, *The Gunfighters, The Old West*. New York: Time-Life Books, 1974, p. 141.

10. Quoted in Trachtman, *The Gunfighters*, p. 149.

11. Quoted in Steve Goldman, "The Hanging Judge," HistoryBuff. www.historybuff.com/library/refhanging.html.

12. Quoted in Jay Robert Nash, ed., *Encyclopedia of Western Lawmen & Outlaws*. New York: Da Capo Press, 1994, p. 252.

13. Quoted in Howard Lamar, ed. *The New Encyclopedia of the American West*. New Haven, CT: Yale University Press, 1998, p. 843.

14. Quoted in "'The Men Who Rode For Parker': Deputy U.S. Marshals and the Federal Court Period in Fort Smith," Fort Smith National Historic Site. www.nps.gov/fosm/history/court/usdm.htm.

15. Quoted in Trachtman, *The Gunfighters*, p. 149.

16. Quoted in Ada Patterson, "An Interview with the Distinguished Jurist by a St. Louis Correspondent," 1896, Fort Smith National Historic Site. www.nps.gov/fosm/history/judgeparker/bio/ada.htm.

17. Quoted in Eric Leonard, "The Speeches of Judge Parker," Fort Smith National Historic Site. www.nps.gov/fosm/history/judgeparker/speeches/cbill2.htm.

18. Quoted in Trachtman, *The Gunfighters*, p. 145.

19. Quoted in David Kopel, "The Self-Defense Cases: How the United States Supreme Court Confronted a Hanging Judge in the Nineteenth Century and Taught Some Lessons for Jurisprudence in the Twenty-First," *American Journal of Criminal Law* Vol. 27 (2000): 296.

20. Quoted in Patterson, "An Interview with the Distinguished Jurist By a St. Louis Correspondent."

Chapter 3: Wyatt Earp: Reluctant Legend

21. Quoted in Stuart N. Lake, *Wyatt Earp, Frontier Marshal*. Boston and New York: Houghton Mifflin, 1931, p. 12.

22. Quoted in Lake, *Wyatt Earp, Frontier Marshal*, p. 65.

23. Quoted in Silva, *Wyatt Earp: A Biography of the Legend*, p. 63.

24. Quoted in Joseph Geringer, "Ellsworth," *Wyatt Earp: Knight with a Six-Shooter*, 2003, Court TV. www.crimelibrary.com/gangsters_outlaws/outlaws/earp/5.html.

25. Quoted in Silva, *Wyatt Earp: A Biography of the Legend*, p. 193.

26. Quoted in Casey Tefetiller, *Wyatt Earp: The Life Behind the Legend*. New York: John Wiley & Sons, 1997, p. 8.

27. Quoted in Joseph Geringer, "Wichita," *Wyatt Earp: Knight with a Six-Shooter*, 2003, Court TV. www.crimelibrary.com/gangsters_outlaws/outlaws/earp/6.html.

28. Quoted in Geringer, "Wichita."

29. Quoted in Joseph Geringer, "Doc Holliday," *Wyatt Earp: Knight with a Six-Shooter*, 2003, Court TV. www.crimelibrary. com/gangsters_outlaws/outlaws/earp/8.html.

30. Masterson, *Famous Gunfighters of the Western Frontier*, p. 46.

31. Josephine Earp, *I Married Wyatt Earp: The Recollections of Josephine Sarah Marcus Earp*, ed. Glenn G. Boyer. Tucson: University of Arizona Press, 1976, p. 28.

32. Quoted in Joseph Geringer, "OK Corral," *Wyatt Earp: Knight with a Six-Shooter*, 2003, Court TV. www.crimelibrary.com/ gangsters_outlaws/outlaws/earp/11.html.

33. Earp, *I Married Wyatt Earp*, p. 121.

Chapter 4: Frank Canton: Alias Joe Horner

34. James D. Horan, *The Authentic Wild West: The Outlaws*. New York: Crown, 1977, p. 233.

35. Quoted in Robert K. DeArment, *Alias Frank Canton*. Norman: University of Oklahoma Press, 1996, p. 31.

36. Quoted in Henry Strong, *My Frontier Days & Indian Fights on the Plains of Texas*. N.P.: n.p., 1926, p. 82.

37. Quoted in DeArment, *Alias Frank Canton*, p. 51.

38. Quoted in "Johnson County War," Wyoming Tales and Trails. www.wyomingtalesandtrails.com/johnson.html.

39. Quoted in Nash, *Encyclopedia of Western Lawmen & Outlaws*, p. 65.

40. Quoted in DeArment, *Alias Frank Canton*, p. 158.

41. Quoted in Roger L. Bell, "Dangerous Dunn Brothers," The Old West Web Ride. www.theoldwestwebride.com/tx1a/dunn.html.

42. Charles F. Colcord, *Autobiography of Charles Francis Colcord, 1859–1934*. Tulsa, OK: C.C. Helmerich, 1970, p. 179.

43. Frank Canton, *Frontier Trails: The Autobiography of Frank Canton*, ed. Everett Dale. Norman: University of Oklahoma Press, 1966, p. 209.

44. Quoted in DeArment, *Alias Frank Canton*, pp. 261–62.

45. Quoted in Charles F. Barrett, "Requiescat en Pace," *Chronicles of Oklahoma* 5, no. 4 (December 1927). http://digital.library. okstate.edu/chronicles/v005/v005p422.html.

Chapter 5: Pat Garrett: Cursed by the Kid

46. Quoted in Leon C. Metz, *Pat Garrett: The Story of a Western Lawman*. Norman: University of Oklahoma Press, 1974, p. 17.

47. Quoted in Trachtman, *The Gunfighters*, p. 190.

48. Quoted in Nash, *Encyclopedia of Western Lawmen & Outlaws*, p. 134.

49. Quoted in Nash, *Encyclopedia of Western Lawmen & Outlaws*, p. 135.

50. Pat Garrett, *The Authentic Life of Billy the Kid*. New York: Indian Head Books, 1994, p. 205.

51. Garrett, *The Authentic Life of Billy the Kid*, p. 216.

52. Quoted in Metz, *Pat Garrett*, p. 121.

53. Garrett, *The Authentic Life of Billy the Kid*, pp. 228–29.

54. Quoted in Leon C. Metz, *The Shooters*. El Paso, TX: Mangan Books, 1976, p. 137.

55. Quoted in Metz, *Pat Garrett*, p. 226.

56. Quoted in Metz, *The Shooters*, p. 149.

57. Quoted in Metz, *The Shooters*, p. 150.

Chapter 6: Bat Masterson: Killer Reputation

58. Quoted in Horan, *The Lawmen*, p. 23.

59. Quoted in Robert K. DeArment, *Bat Masterson, The Man and the Legend*. Norman: University of Oklahoma Press, 1979, p. 80.

60. Quoted in Trachtman, *The Gunfighters*, p. 122.

61. DeArment, *Bat Masterson*, p. 159.

62. Quoted in Trachtman, *The Gunfighters*, p. 124.

63. Quoted in Nash, *Encyclopedia of Western Lawmen & Outlaws*, p. 228.

64. Quoted in DeArment, *Bat Masterson*, p. 377.

65. Quoted in Trachtman, *The Gunfighters*, p. 35

66. Quoted in Joseph G. Rosa, *The Gunfighter: Man or Myth?* Norman: University of Oklahoma Press, 1969, p. 122.

67. Bat Masterson, *Famous Gunfighters of the Western Frontier*, p. 9.

68. Quoted in DeArment, *Bat Masterson*, pp. 396–97.

Chapter 7: Bill Tilghman: Last of the Frontier Lawmen

69. Masterson, *Famous Gunfighters of the Western Frontier*, p. 47.

70. Quoted in Floyd Miller, *Bill Tilghman: Marshal of the Last Frontier*. Garden City, NY: Doubleday, 1968, p. 68.

71. Quoted in Miller, *Bill Tilghman*, p. 84.

72. Quoted in Miller, *Bill Tilghman*, p. 84.

73. Quoted in Juliet Galonska, "Myths?" Fort Smith National Historic Site, March 1996. www.nps.gov/fosm/history/radio/32.htm.

74. Quoted in Trachtman, *The Gunfighters*, p. 160.

75. Quoted in Harry C. Buffardi, "William 'Bill' Tilghman." *The History of the Office of Sheriff*, 1998. New York Correction History Society. www.correctionhistory.org/html/chronicl/sheriff/ch18.htm.

76. Quoted in Horan, *The Lawmen*, p. 174.

77. Quoted in "Tilghman, Noted Peace Officer, Here," *Oklahoma Leader*, July 20, 1916, Logan County Researchers Homepage. http://homepages.rootsweb.com/~tammie/law/tilghman peace.htm.

78. Quoted in "Bill Tilghman," El Buscaderos—Cowboy Action Shooting, May 1998. www.netw.com/cowboy/_feature/feature 0598.html.

79. Quoted in "Community Events," Tulsa World, October 11, 2003. http://www.tulsaworld.com/cals/CEVNT/eventView.phtml?Event_ID=9195.

FOR FURTHER READING

Books

Kent Alexander, *Heroes of the Wild West*. New York: Mallard Press, 1992. Written for younger readers, this volume is an excellent introduction to many of the legends of the western frontier.

Harry Sinclair Drago, *The Legend Makers: Tales of the Old-Time Peace Officers and Desperados of the Frontier*. New York: Dodd, Mead, 1975. A respected Old West historian's perspective on several well-known and lesser-known lawmen and outlaws, this volume includes chapters on the Earp and Masterson brothers, Pat Garrett, and several others, as well as several rare photographs.

Richard Mancini, *American Legends of the Wild West*. Philadelphia: Courage Books, 1992. An oversized picture book, this impressive book contains a huge array of photographs with accompanying text.

Thomas Thrasher, *Gunfighters of the American West*, History Makers. San Diego, CA: Lucent, 2000. An interesting book in the History Makers series that includes separate chapters on Wyatt Earp and Wild Bill Hickok.

Frank Waters, *The Earp Brothers of Tombstone: The Story of Mrs. Virgil Earp*. New York: C.N. Potter, 1960. The story of the Earp brothers told from the point of view of Virgil Earp's wife, this book shows Wyatt Earp in a most negative light.

Web sites

HistoryBuff (www.historybuff.com). Quick reference material for term papers and essays on any subject matter can be found at this site, which includes reprinted articles and essays.

Oldwest.com (www.oldwest.com). Every known Web site involving the Old West can be found by logging on and going through the many links categorized by subject matter.

Tulsaworld.com (www.tulsaworld.com). Tulsa's official site has links and articles about Oklahoma's historical and current events.

WORKS CONSULTED

Books

Allen Barra, *Inventing Wyatt Earp: His Life and Many Legends.* New York: Carroll & Graf, 1998. This book takes in the many elements of the Earp legend and shows it to be largely untrue, but the author's reasoning is questionable. Great photos include images of Earp in popular culture.

Frank Canton, *Frontier Trails: The Autobiography of Frank Canton,* edited by Everett Dale. Norman: University of Oklahoma Press, 1966. Canton's own version of his life makes for interesting reading but downplays the less savory aspects of his years as outlaw Joe Horner.

Charles F. Colcord, *Autobiography of Charles Francis Colcord, 1859–1934.* Tulsa, OK: C.C. Helmerich, 1970. Firsthand account of this frontier lawman's experiences, this book includes an interesting portrait of Frank Canton/Joe Horner.

Robert K. DeArment, *Bat Masterson, The Man and The Legend.* Norman: University of Oklahoma Press, 1979. Excellent research and comprehensive analysis on the title subject highlight this biography, which also includes many rare photographs, notes, and an extensive bibliography.

————, *Alias Frank Canton.* Norman: University of Oklahoma Press, 1996. Fascinating reading, this biography is the most definitive on Canton. Rare photos are included throughout the text.

Robert R. Dykstra, *The Cattle Towns.* New York: Knopf, 1968. The author of this book is a renowned historian who approaches his subject with insight and presents it with rare photos.

Josephine Earp, *I Married Wyatt Earp: The Recollections of Josephine Sarah Marcus Earp,* edited by Glenn G. Boyer. Tucson: University of Arizona Press, 1976. This autobiography by Josie Earp is annotated greatly by editor Glenn Boyer.

Pat Garrett, *The Authentic Life of Billy The Kid.* New York: Indian Head Books, 1994. Garrett's version of the life of Billy the Kid is largely ghostwritten until chapter sixteen, when the reader gets a firsthand account of Garrett's own run-in with the Kid.

James D. Horan, *The Authentic Wild West: The Lawmen.* New York: Crown, 1980. One in a three-volume work documenting the lawmen of the Old West with extremely rare photos and chapters on, among others, Bat Masterson, Bear River Tom Smith, Bill Tilghman, and Wyatt Earp.

————, *The Authentic Wild West: The Outlaws.* New York: Crown, 1977. Part of a three-volume work on the Old West that includes rare photos and chapters on Billy the Kid and several others.

Stuart N. Lake, *Wyatt Earp, Frontier Marshal.* Boston and New York: Houghton Mifflin, 1931. This is the authorized biography of Wyatt Earp, which helped to create his legendary status.

Howard Lamar, ed., *The New Encyclopedia of the American West.* New Haven, CT: Yale University Press, 1998. This massive reference book contains alphabetized entries that encompass every conceivable aspect of the American West.

Bat Masterson, *Famous Gunfighters of the Western Frontier.* Olympic Valley, CA: Outbooks, 1978. The author's sketches are more fiction than fact, but they illustrate Masterson's writing ability. Includes chapters about Wyatt Earp, Bill Tilghman, and others, with illustrations by Frederick Remington.

Leon C. Metz, *Pat Garrett: The Story of a Western Lawman.* Norman: University of Oklahoma Press, 1974. The best biography on this subject, Garrett is presented honestly, as is the time in which he lived. Contains several rare photos.

————, *The Shooters.* El Paso, TX: Mangan Books, 1976. This renowned author encapsulates the careers of almost two dozen legendary gunmen in individual chapters, including lawmen Tom Smith, Pat Garrett, and Wyatt Earp. A highlight is the detailed bibliography.

Floyd Miller, *Bill Tilghman: Marshal of the Last Frontier.* Garden City, NY: Doubleday, 1968. This biography is written in narrative form and reads almost like a novel. Includes many rare photos.

Jay Robert Nash, ed., *Encyclopedia of Western Lawmen & Outlaws.* New York: Da Capo Press, 1994. This impressive oversized book contains biographical entries of all the legendary lawmen and many rare photographs.

Joseph G. Rosa, *The Gunfighter: Man or Myth?* Norman: University of Oklahoma Press, 1969. This scholarly, critical analysis of the gunfighter phenomenon contains several photos.

Lee A. Silva, *Wyatt Earp: A Biography of the Legend,* vol. 1, *The Cowtown Years.* Santa Ana, CA: Graphic Publishers, 2002. This glossy-paged epic encompasses the subject's life up to his days in Dodge City by combining previously published and unpublished material with an updated narrative text. Includes many rare and never-before-published photographs as well as several detailed notes and bibliographies.

Floyd B. Streeter, *Prairie Trails & Cow Towns: The Opening of the Old West*. New York: Devin Adair, 1963. The renowned Kansas historian meticulously details the economic and historic significance of the Kansas cow towns on the western frontier.

Henry Strong, *My Frontier Days & Indian Fights on the Plains of Texas*. N.P.: n.p., 1926. The author details his life as a lawman in Texas, which includes his near-deadly run-in with the Joe Horner Gang.

Casey Tefertiller, *Wyatt Earp: The Life Behind the Legend*. New York: Wiley, 1997. One of several well-researched biographies to be published in the last few years that reaffirms Earp's legacy as a lawman. Well-documented bibliography and photos.

Paul Trachtman, *The Gunfighters, The Old West*. New York: Time-Life Books, 1974. The volume in the Time-Life Old West series that comes closest to dealing with the western lawman. Profusely illustrated with intelligent and anecdote-laden text.

Roger H. Tuller, *Let No Guilty Man Escape: A Judicial Biography of "Hanging Judge" Isaac C. Parker*. Norman: University of Oklahoma Press, 2001. This biography of Parker concentrates mainly on his judicial career from a legal point of view.

Periodicals

Allen Barra, "Who Was Wyatt Earp?" *American Heritage*, December 1998.

Hubert I. Cohen, "Wyatt Earp at the OK Corral," *Journal of American Culture*, June 2003.

Michael Janofsky, "122 Years Later Lawmen Are Still Chasing Billy the Kid," *New York Times*, June 5, 2003.

David Kopel, "The Self-Defense Cases: How the United States Supreme Court Confronted a Hanging Judge in the Nineteenth Century and Taught Some Lessons for Jurisprudence in the Twenty-First." *American Journal of Criminal Law* (2000).

Christopher Sharrett, "Apocalypse at the O.K. Corral," *USA Today Magazine*, January 1995.

Internet Sources

Charles F. Barrett, "Requiescat en Pace," *Chronicles of Oklahoma* 5, no. 4 (December 1927). http://digital.library.okstate.edu/chronicles/ v005/v005p422.html.

Roger L. Bell, "Dangerous Dunn Brothers," The Old West Web Ride. www.theoldwestwebride.com/tx1a/dunn.html.

"Bill Tilghman," El Buscaderos—Cowboy Action Shooting, May 1998. www.netw.com/cowboy/_feature/feature0598.html.

Harry C. Buffardi, *The History of the Office of Sheriff*, 1998, New York Correction History Society. www.correctionhistory.org/html/chronicl/ sheriff/toc.htm.

Juliet Galonska, "Myths?" Fort Smith National Historic Site, March 1996. www.nps.gov/fosm/history/radio/32.htm.

Joseph Geringer, *Wyatt Earp: Knight with a Six-Shooter*, 2003, Court TV. www.crimelibrary.com/gangsters_outlaws/outlaws/earp/1.html.

Steve Goldman, "The Hanging Judge," History Buff. www.historybuff. com/library/refhanging.html.

"Johnson County War," Wyoming Tails and Trails. www.wyoming talesandtrails.com/johnson.html.

Gregory Lalire, "The Lip of The Law," The Old West Web Ride. www .theoldwestwebride.com.

Eric Leonard, "Biography of Judge Parker," 2002, Fort Smith National Historic Site. www.nps.gov/fosm/history/judgeparker/bio/.

————, "The Speeches of Judge Parker," Fort Smith National Historic Site. www.nps.gov/fosm/history/judgeparker/speeches /cbill2.htm.

"'The Men Who Rode for Parker': Deputy U.S. Marshals and the Federal Court Period in Fort Smith," 2002, Fort Smith National Historic Site. www.nps.gov/fosm/history/court/usdm.htm.

Patterson, Ada, "An Interview with the Distinguished Jurist by a St. Louis Correspondent," 1896, Fort Smith National Historic Site. www.nps.gov/fosm/history/judgeparker/bio/ada.htm.

"Tilghman, Noted Peace Officer, Here," *Oklahoma Leader*, July 20, 1916, Logan County Researchers Homepage. http://home pages.roots web.com/~tammie/law/tilghmanpeace.htm.

"The Wild West," June 1997. www.gunslinger.com/west.html.

INDEX

PICTURE CREDITS

ABOUT THE AUTHOR

Dwayne Epstein was born in Brooklyn, New York, and grew up
in Southern California. He first wrote professionally in 1982,
writing newspaper film reviews and year-end analysis of popular
culture. Nationally, he has been a regular contributor to several
film magazines since 1996. Internationally, he contributed to Bill
Krohn's *Serious Pleasures*, which was published in Europe in
1997. Mr. Epstein has published several children's books since
2000 and is currently writing a biography on the actor Lee Mar-
vin. Mr. Epstein also wrote *People In the News: Adam Sandler* for
Lucent Books. He lives in Long Beach with his girlfriend, Barbara,
and too many books on movie history.